EX-LIBRIS

Anne Duck

Eskimo Parish

Eskimo Parish

By PAUL O'CONNOR, S.J.

THE BRUCE PUBLISHING COMPANY
MILWAUKEE

Nihil obstat: JOHN A. SCHULIEN, Censor librorum
Imprimatur: ✠ MOYSES E. KILEY, Archiepiscopus Milwaukiensis
September 4, 1946

Foreword

SPRING in Alaska!

The smell of burning brush, the sound of hammer and saw thin on the clear spring air, the patched white and brown of the thawing river bank, and three men, grunting over heavy timbers. Log on log was labored into place, and the walls rose higher and higher. Then the beams, and the earth roof. The door was hung and an altar raised. And Christ came to dwell in the first Jesuit church, built by Fathers Tosi and Robaut, and Brother Giordano at Nulato in 1888.

From that spring almost sixty years ago to the present the work of the men of Ignatius has gone on. During that time over one hundred Jesuits have dedicated their lives and toil to the work of the Alaskan Mission. From one log cabin, twenty by thirty feet, have sprung over fifty mission centers at the cost of incalculable effort and sacrifice.

From one infant baptized on the bleak hillside of an Aleutian island in 1759, to literally hundreds of children in Sisters' schools and homes. From one mass celebrated in the chill unfriendliness of Fort Yukon in 1862, a symphony of adoration and of praise is raised daily to the Father from all parts of Alaska. From the one martyrdom offered so gladly by the great Archbishop Seghers that same year have blossomed scores of lives, each offered as gladly. Christ, Who once shivered almost alone, now has company in hundreds of out of the way places in the land that still is shrouded in mystery and danger.

It was this growing life in the north that caught the attention of the young Paul O'Connor. He was born and educated in

Spokane, Washington, and early came into contact with the Jesuits of the Northwest. And almost as early his eyes and heart turned north. He joined the Society of Jesus in 1915 and spent the next fifteen years in pointed and quite deliberate preparation for the work he could see ahead.

And then in 1930 he left for the north. For the first three years he became the "Lord's Tramp of the Tundra," moving about through the numberless native villages that lie in the vicinity of Holy Cross and Mountain Village.

Then followed a period in and around Akulurak. His remarkable physique made it possible for him to travel, by dogsled in winter and boat in summer, more extensively perhaps than any missionary in Alaska.

He has spent the last five years at Kotzebue, where the Arctic circle is something at which you point south; where the Bering Sea is something you watch with careful dread lest it suddenly rise up and kill.

These sixteen years, packed as they were with danger and adventure, drollery and warming accomplishment, were important in themselves. But when the man who lived them can also capture them and distill them in words for the purpose of sharing them with others — that is in a certain sense even more important. For every word has the urgency of personal experience, and every experience has a significance infinitely more widespread than the individual detail that makes it up.

And, since the author of this recounting of gripping experiences and lucid insights is a man who has found that Christ is more important than himself, he has managed to reveal little of what it has cost him to help the life of Christ to grow. Nor is there much directly said about all his great brothers in Christ who have preceded and accompanied him on this quest for the Eternal Grail. All that is understood, however, thrumming a clear undertone in everything he has written. Father Paul O'Connor would be the first man to admit that it is only by standing on the shoulders of giants that he has been able to light another candle on the high altar of Alaska.

His book is designed according to these larger chronological divisions: the time he spent at Mountain Village, at Akulurak, and at Kotzebue; but it is not, strictly speaking, a history. It is rather a work of art, in the sense that the stories, movements, personalities, all of them true in themselves, are arranged in a giant, complicated symbol, portraying for the reader the intangible reality of the soul of the North. For it is a story of great souls; those who have gone before him; the dramatic struggle of a missionary for the soul of his people; and the gradual, absorbing revelation of the soul of a little-known civilization.

And above all it is a story of the soul of Christ as that soul expands and grows, to include in its quiet joy that strange land of darkness and light, of chill and warmth, of stars and storms. For it is, in the final analysis, only that soul that can give proper sense to the apparently senseless sacrifices made by these men of God who give so much that many can live the life of God.

THOMAS L. O'BRIEN, S.J.

Alma College,
Alma, California

Contents

1. Tundra Sick Call . . .

MEASLES had struck on the Yukon Delta. I had been in Alaska only a short time, and had the job of a wandering minstrel of the north, visiting innumerable out-of-the-way cabins and villages. By some means or other the vicious little bug was discharged by some careless freighter at one of his stops. Contact was immediately made with the neighboring village, and the siege was on. No village was too tiny or too hidden away to escape. Dusky Eskimo faces grew feverishly red. Doctors seemed helpless, so the natives dusted off their traditional medicine men; but even these dark practitioners were powerless. The disease, really dangerous because of poor conditions, moved on and on, missing only the very aged. Newborn babies were almost certainly doomed. Slowly, implacably, the toll of the dead mounted.

The wave of disease swept inexorably down into the territory I was working. Suddenly I found myself in the midst of many sick people, most of whom were panicky and bewildered besides being ill.

As you know, one of the most difficult, and most consoling jobs the priest has is attending the sick. It is difficult because there is so much fear and suffering connected with it. And most priests are human enough to experience a sympathetic vibration at other's pain. It is consoling because we approach a sickbed usually after everything else had failed. The priest begins where every human help leaves off. To stand above the sick and watch the taut lines of fear and dread dissolve into a smile of peace;

1

to watch haunted eyes gradually grow light with hope — that is consolation worthy of the name.

The Alaskan priest is no exception. Work with the sick up here is proportionately more difficult, and more consoling. Merely the physical job of getting to the sick is often enough almost prohibitive, if only there were not a soul in need. But the translucent childlikeness of the natives in pain, their quick response to things spiritual at such a time, these turn the sobering work of attending the sick into a real joy.

Before long the entire Akulurak Mission was afflicted with measles. By some strange quirk it missed the Fathers and Sisters, leaving them to care for the ninety sick children. Because of that care the sick were saved, but the effects of the epidemic were apparent for months to come. The weakness which followed gave new life to the tuberculosis germs that are always near the top in the Eskimo system. Hacking coughs and frightening exhaustion followed throughout the rest of the year.

But the real sadness came in the lonely little villages on the tundra. Frequently I would come in off the trail and stop at a lone igloo to find the whole family in bed, no food in the house, and not a stick of wood or drop of oil for fuel.

One time I was making one of my usual missionary round trips and came upon two hunters on their trap lines. Since a storm was rising, we lined our three teams up and raced for the nearest village. I shall not soon forget the feeling of eerie fear and awe that rose up within me when I saw the silently huddled huts in a distance. Not a sign of life did we see.

"*Yuitok!*" (nobody home!) shouted one of my hunter companions. But somehow I knew better. We swept up in a rush and stopped. There beside the nearest igloo were a dozen half-starved dogs chained to their stakes. I moved into the cabin and found the whole family in bed. There was little food, no fuel.

The place was a shambles; dirty dishes, littered floor, mukluks and winter gear scattered everywhere, and the smell! My hunter friends departed to get wood while I cleaned the place a bit, started some food cooking, and prepared and anointed three people for death. I was sorry to leave because these poor natives badly needed further help, but I knew that sickness lay ahead of me too. The weak, brave smiles of gratitude from these people whom we found in gloom and left in relative comfort were enough to make the next leg of my journey somehow warmer than I had expected.

I was gone only an hour or so on my way to the next village when the fog suddenly rolled in from the sea. I took compass direction from the sun before it was completely blotted out, and headed my dogs over toward the willow-tangled banks of the Black River. This would lead me to my next stop.

Breaking brush for half a mile with a long string of eleven Malemutes is a patient and draining task. With almost satanic perversity the dogs continued to wrap their harness lines around a willow, and end up face to face with some little-loved companion. And then the fun started.

But it is only fun in retrospect. In the midst of cottony fog, gathering darkness, meshlike willows, tangled harness, and snarling, fighting dogs there is no fun. I finally broke through the brush, however, and got onto the river itself. Then through the foggy blackness I went on, hugging the bank of the river literally for dear life. I knew that it would bring me to the next village.

Two more hours of mushing blindly finally brought me to my destination. I found only two people up and about, a little boy and his older sister, both under fifteen. They had been heroically caring for two large families alone. Here I repeated my work; helped to clean up, gathered some extra fuel, fixed up two marriages, baptized a baby, anointed one man. I stayed there all night, and the next morning was very happy to let the glory of the Mass sift through all that suffering and fear, and leave a wonderful peace where there had been a dark sadness before.

That day was crystal clear and very cold. I lost no time getting to my next village, and was agreeably surprised to find everyone well and brimming with Alaskan sunshine. Several of these people were old school children, and they gladdened my trip with their joy and downright simple piety. Some hunters came in that night, and the next morning I had quite a congregation for Mass.

It was two weeks before I returned to my headquarters musing thoughtfully on the childlike qualities of my people. They are not afraid to die; they are terribly susceptible to sickness, pitifully inept at handling epidemics — and yet they have a strong man's patience and courage in the face of suffering itself.

Two days later I received word that another village was stricken, so I started out again. My route lay somewhere near the cabin of an old couple named Adam and Eve. Adam, I knew, had been sick for a month, so I decided to look in on him if possible. By that time it was getting late in the season, so we had to watch the weather closely.

Dawn was just breaking as we pushed our heavily loaded sled toward the dog boxes. Every Malemute there, a little rested after his late trip, strained against their chains at the sight of the sled. With the help of several of the mission boys I quickly slipped the harness on, hooked up the sled, loosened the towline, and dashed off into the misty morning. The dogs were excited and ran frantically, dragging the sled from one harsh bump to the next. I expected a crash at any minute but we managed to keep the sled upright and on the trail. Dogs will usually quiet down after a few hundred yards of this initial dash, but in this case there was another team up ahead, and my dogs had the scent. There is no use arguing with them; they will keep this pace until the team is overtaken and passed.

After an hour of fast going we passed a little village of four cabins. I knew that there was no sickness there, so a wave of the hand to some playing children, and we were gone.

We hit an unbroken trail then, and running through deep snow took my attention and strength for the next half hour. Then we dropped down onto a slough that had been swept clean by the wind. It was good traveling. We swept up to another little place with two houses. I stopped to "breathe" the dogs and visit one of the old mission boys who had been wasting away from consumption. He greeted me with a smile (after three months in bed), and assured me that he would soon be on his trap line again. I visited briefly with him, got directions for reaching Adam and Eve's cabin, and left.

This time my leader, Berry, waited for directions. After the next three hours of wandering I began to get that indefinable twitch that usually means you are lost. I was thinking uncomfortably about spending the night on the open tundra, when I spied a hunter in the distance. I "gee'd" my dogs over to him, and was delighted to find that he was an old friend of mine, a reindeer herder. He told me that we would never find Adam's cabin in the dark, and suggested that we spend the night with him.

So a few minutes later we sat down gratefully to a steaming reindeer supper. Rosary and instruction followed, and then the sleeping bag. It had been a hard day, and the next would be harder, if you could judge from the storm outside at the moment.

After Mass the following day we left, with good directions and deep snow underfoot. That meant a lot of heavy trail work, pushing the sled and wading through deep drifts. Progress was slow and painful. Lunch was a half dozen dried figs taken on the fly. A little later a snowstorm came up and I began to get apprehensive. I still don't like the idea of making the open tundra my home for a night. It would be easy to grow panicky under these conditions, because the problem of keeping from freezing to death between 3:30 p.m. when darkness falls and 9:00 a.m. the next morning is no small one. And from the looks of things, the next day was going to be worse.

Our Lady of the Snows is a very kind Lady, though. I let her know about things through a *Memorare*, and switched the dogs back over a long lake. Within ten minutes they picked up their pace significantly and suddenly swung around onto a barely discernible trail. We swung along over the fast-disappearing trail, both dogs and men quickened by the prospect of shelter. Then we began to smell smoke through the swirling snow and falling dark, and before long we stood before the half-buried igloo of Adam.

I stooped and entered the little home to find this ancient of the North stretched out on his last sickbed. We talked briefly, and then we prepared the dogs for the night and brought in our bedding. We had had no hot food for over six hours, so a cup of tea was very welcome. I gave Adam a long instruction on the sacrament of Extreme Unction, then sent the others out into the storm shed while I heard his confession. Then the last sacrament followed with impressive solemnity in that tiny house.

After this Adam felt in an expansive mood, so we sat for an hour or so listening to him tell of the time when there were no whites in Alaska and when the Innuit warred with the Malemute. The next morning I said Mass with my six-foot height stooped into five. A light breakfast and off we went, into a raging blizzard.

I had asked Adam's boy if he knew the way to the next village, and he assured me that his dogs could find the trail in any weather, so we headed down the storm with the wind at our backs. The flying snow whirled around our parka hoods. At times I had a strange feeling that the team ahead was lost forever. But my own leader would never let the other dogs get away from him, so we moved silently through the blinding snow without a worry in the world.

At noon we pulled up beside another of those lonely little cabins of the tundra. I found a little baby Eskimo girl with the measles. I baptized her and prepared her for heaven, where she would be before I had long been gone.

We were still a half day away from the stricken village though, so we left again to repeat the morning's performance. At dusk we arrived finally, to find practically the whole village down. I spent the rest of the evening preparing three people for death and baptizing another little girl. The clean-up job was pretty stiff, but with the help of my own guide and several of the villagers, we got things in good order. That night I heard the confessions of all who were well in preparation for Mass and Communion the next morning.

After Mass, I waded through deep snow, bringing Holy Viaticum to the dying people whom I had anointed the night before. That day the wind had veered around and was coming from the south. That meant slushy weather and dangerous sloughs, so we headed for a mission station forty miles away instead of directly back to headquarters. There we waited for a freeze, and hurried home without further incident.

That freeze held very well for that time of the year. So, after a few days of rest for both men and dogs, I decided to visit my stations upriver. The farthest station in that direction was only one hundred miles away, and the trail was ideal. So with a refreshed team and a native boy as guide we left the village and swept over the wind-swept trail.

After an hour or so I gave the handle bars to my guide and settled back in the sled for a swift, invigorating ride. I was just beginning to think that this Alaskan missionary life wasn't so bad after all when I noticed a slight change in the wind. I remarked casually to my guide that it might have been better to have started this trip a day or so earlier. And I was right! For the wind shifted due south.

Slicing rain followed within a matter of minutes. Off came my fur parka, on went the rainproof one. The rain fell in rivers. Snow disappeared before my eyes. Huge drifts turned into soggy masses of slush. It was impossible to turn back; impossible to get any wetter. The wind and rain were thawing everything in sight except me; wearing wet clothes next to my skin was not exactly the most comfortable way to be clad, even in a south wind.

My guide in the meantime had made only one remark — "*anoklirtok*" (it's windy).

We continued to travel swiftly, however, as the bumps along the ice had been smoothed by the thaw. We overtook and passed the crack sixteen-dog mail team, and finally arrived at my station. A siege of whooping cough had broken out, and many of the young mothers who had never seen such a thing before were on the verge of panic. I spent a busy two days passing out medicine, and assuring the worried parents that there was nothing to fear. But I was very glad that I had arrived when I did, for this little village had been too close to panic. It helped them to see that I was not worried about their condition. I waited for one of those quick winter freezes, and got home again without any further trouble.

2. I Was in Prison and . . .

THERE is perhaps no freer man on earth than the tundra Eskimo; and yet few are more enslaved. The days and nights are theirs to use as they choose; distances are only to be traveled. Skies, fresh air, food for the taking, all these surround them with the necessary physical equipment for freedom. And yet the very distances that give them freedom also imprison them; the food and clothing that waits to be taken from the land chains them down. The skies themselves that can be so penetratingly blue can also forge stormy bonds of restraint more binding than any steel. The land with its width and breadth and depth gives freedom to the physical man, but builds up inexorably the walls of the prison of the spirit.

That is why it is so necessary for the priest in Alaska to make many visits to his people; he must do everything to break through those spiritual prison walls, and bring freedom to the distant ones, the ones who are free to eat, but seldom free to love God.

I began to prepare for my last long trip of the late winter season. The dogs were hardened by the long travel of the winter. This trip was to go up to the Kussilvak Mountains and the Black River district with its numerous lakes and widely scattered villages.

These mountains serve the musher both as a guide and a barometer. The Eskimo can gauge unerringly where he is merely by the contours of the hills nearest him; he can foresee the next day's weather by the formation of clouds hanging about the

ps. In March and April when the day stretches long
ght, fantastic mirages rise up around the heights.
they are towering citadels, sometimes great cathe-
___g to the skies; and sometimes the mountains them-
selves get up and walk. And that panorama occurs to every
traveler, not only to those who have spent a month by themselves
on the empty trail.

Banjo, Ukulele, Saxophone, Monkey, Pepper, Scotty, Uzok,
and Stick-in-the-Mud, with Berry at the lead spot, tugged at the
towline. My fur-swathed two hundred pounds was bearing down
on the brake. The Eskimo boy with a nod from me and a
"*Upskena*" (get ready), loosed the towline.

Over the tundra we flew, bouncing from one rise to another
until I began to wish longingly for balloon-tired sleds. From the
tundra we dropped down to an inland lake, swept smooth as
glass by the play of winds from every direction. It was there that
I breathed a prayer of gratitude for the ingenuity and thought-
fulness of the mission Brother who had installed an ice brake on
my sled. Without it I would have been swinging back and forth
behind the dogs like the tail of a kite.

With the wind behind us we swept out onto Kimlih lake. Just
about four miles from home the Kimlih broadened into almost
an inland sea. I was just rejoicing at our auspicious beginnings
when I heard the rumble of the cracking tide ice. I yelled at the
dogs — but was just too late. The heavy sled dropped into a
foot of water and settled as if for life. But after a half hour of
pulling and hauling, geeing, hawing, and splashing through icy
waters, we finally got out and on our way again. Fortunately
it wasn't too cold, only eight above zero, so I could keep my
soaked feet from freezing by running the hour or so that divided
us from the first native cabin.

Wet feet on the trail can become very disagreeable. However, on this occasion I soon reached a clean cabin belonging to two of our old mission children and was well cared for. My boots were pulled off while I sipped steaming coffee; fresh straw was inserted, and they were hung up to dry. I dug out dry socks from my bag, and was set again for the trail.

At 11:30 a.m. I was off over an unmarked country heading straight for the mountains. After an hour or so of mushing I saw a black fox about two hundred yards away curiously speculating on the dogs in their harness. I stepped on the brake, but the wise little fellow was off before I could reach for my rifle. Just beyond this point we had a dangerous slide down a bank onto a lake. Halfway down my dogs spied a mink, and off they went, yelping with delight. I put all my weight on the brake, but there might as well have been none. The dogs sped across the lake after the frightened mink that fortunately disappeared down a hole just in time. I veered the dogs off to the left with a raucous "haw," and proceeded to pick up my trail again.

Around 4:00 p.m. the sky began to darken. It would be night before six o'clock. I had to hurry if I wanted to escape the doubtful pleasure of a night bivouac on the trail. Just at six o'clock we slipped down onto the Nantivik Slough and found our bearings. We could follow this ice no matter how dark it grew. A long way from my first village, the dogs caught the scent of their husky brothers ahead. With a burst of unexpected speed after the hard day, they swept us into the village for which we had been looking.

Nantivik consists of two habitations, one a log cabin and the other a dugout. I handed my dogs over to one of the boys and prospected a bit before deciding where to settle for the night. The cabin looked promising from the outside, but when I had pushed my way in, I found no less than twelve people packed into surroundings that would make the clean cold of the trail something ardently to be desired. I greeted them all cordially, and after a few words left and went over to the dugout. I found it clean; only three people lived here. This, I decided, would be my resting place for the night.

On these trips I usually go pretty well stocked with food. The Eskimos will give you what they have, but this may be anything from an eel to an odorous muskrat. On this occasion, however, I was treated to a feast of arctic hare. I seasoned the cooking myself so the meal turned out quite palatable. As a rule the man in from the trail can eat anything with relish. I have stored away beaver and porcupine after nine hours of travel and found them tasty beyond my dreams. Off the trail, though, I must confess that I am a little more circumspect.

After supper I gave the current news of the trail, spoke of the fur that was plentiful that year, and then prepared for a short instruction. Afterward rosary and confessions. The night was spent on the dirt floor. Mice were as thick as flies that year, but for once I wasn't much bothered by them. Some nights they actually presumed on the warmth of my sleeping bag.

I was up at four-thirty and by five-fifteen was saying Mass in the packed little dugout. The Holy Sacrifice has its own grandeur no matter what the surroundings. Each time I celebrate Mass in these low, dark, humble dugouts, I think of the Christ Child's manger, and feel better about calling Him down to such an inglorious place. There is something that is somehow pre-eminently fitting in this ultimate humiliation of His.

At seven o'clock I was off again in the cold, penetrating air of morning. Luckily I had a local boy going my way to visit his traps. By noon we were at the foot of the mountains. A fox stood still for two shots, but the distance was too great for success. The lakes at the foot of these mountains are always swept with winds, and at that time had open water in them. Attention

during the next few hours was going to be strictly on mushing.
We finally rounded the mountain and slipped down to the Black
River. Here the team ahead of me came near to a cold bath.
Quick action by the musher saved all but two dogs from a ducking. The leader and swing dog went down, but managed to
scramble back on solid ice. After a full ten hours on the trail we
finally reached our destination too tired to think of anything but
hot food and a warm bear rug.

I had planned to spend only the morning at this little place,
taking up the time with Mass and the sacraments, instructions,
and rosary. But when morning came, it brought one of the late
winter *chinooks* that mushers dread so much. Here I was, stuck
at this out-of-the-way place, wondering if I could possibly get
back to my headquarters on schedule. However, warm weather
doesn't last long in the Alaskan winter, so before nightfall that
day it started to freeze again. The next morning I was up and
on the trail by five o'clock. I had a long haul to Mountain
Village on the Yukon. It was still dark the next morning when
the big mail team swept down the Yukon with its brakes scream-
ing. These mail teams are invariably crack outfits, consisting of
from eleven to fifteen magnificent dogs. It paused very briefly,
and then with a mighty swerve moved back on the Yukon ice
and was gone in the darkness. I had not had a chance to prepare
my own team, so the process of harnessing eleven quiveringly
anxious dogs went on in the chill dark. It was only forty-five
minutes later that we finally straightened out the snarling dogs
and dashed away in yelping pursuit of the mail. Only a mighty
heave by my guide saved us from an ugly spill as we cleared
the bank down to the river.

It was two solid hours of speedy travel before we came in
sight of the mail. In the meantime, a friend of mine, Charlie
Peterson, with his seven lanky huskies and light sled had over-

taken me. At last we caught the mail at lunch time and rested
for an hour. Each husky was given a bite of frozen fish. On the
trail they are never fed much; they don't need it, for a mouthful
at noon puts new blood in their veins.

The mail sled left first. In a swish it vanished around the curve
in the river. Charlie Peterson then lifted his brake and away he
went. A moment later I was in the race. As I rounded the bend
I noticed that both sleds ahead were swerving back and forth
across the ice. I thanked God and the brother again for the ice
brake which kept me on a beeline for my destination. The other
team cut in behind me, and for the next hour we were a caravan
across the ice.

We were about a quarter of a mile ahead of the mail team
when I discovered a bad mistake. We were behind a sandy little
island that had been swept clean of snow. The wind had blown
the sand in generous drifts across the ice at this point, and we
were caught. Twenty dogs couldn't pull a heavy sled over sand.
Suddenly we saw the barest ribbon of a clear trail on the left
side of the river. We swung over and found smooth going for
almost a mile.

I looked back then, and saw the mail sled stuck like a boat
on a sand bar. I silently congratulated myself on the good fortune of discovering the difficulty early enough to do something
about it. We, who had started out to follow the mail sled down
the river finally led it into the next stop by a full hour.

Here I heard of a newborn baby and a sick woman several
days' run off my route, so I decided to take the detour and do
what I could for them. I left early the next morning, hoping
to use as much of the ice as possible before the morning thaw
might start. It was getting late in the year, and the trail was
dependable up to nine-thirty in the morning. After that, it was
luck. The ice on the river had become brittle, and I wasn't more

than two hours on the trail before I had to put moccasins on the dogs' feet. Dog moccasins are made from outing flannel to fit their paws. It is a heart-rending sight for any dog lover to see a long red trail stretch out behind his team of bleeding dogs. Sometimes, in spite of the best calculations, you find yourself a long way from home with only a few tattered moccasins left. Dogs will lose them on a slushy trail, or on water-covered ice.

Things went well that day. A north wind sprang up and kept the trail fairly hard during the entire run. I baptized the baby, heard many confessions, and gave Communion to a group of fervent Eskimos. The second day it began to rain and before I reached one of my little chapels on the banks of the Yukon my dogs looked like huge, dank muskrats, and the feet of every one of them were bleeding profusely. The ice, too, was beginning to get soggy and dangerous. The third day I gave Viaticum to the sick woman. It was still raining and mushing became nothing but literal "mushing" through rotten ice and over snowless sand bars.

The fourth day I said Mass at midnight and was on the trail in the dark at 2:45 a.m. It was raining and the sky was overcast. On account of the overflow I had to make a long detour. In the darkness and rain I missed a small slough that I was supposed to enter from the Yukon and lost a precious hour splashing through almost knee-deep water looking for it. What made me more than usually provoked at myself was the fact that if I had followed the directions of my leader, Berry, I would never have gone off the trail.

I waded across a small stream that reached the top of my hip boots, and then called the dogs over. For some two hours I hugged the sandbank of a stream that was filled with floating ice. When I finally reached the lower fork of the Yukon my dogs were black with mud and so was I. I was soaking — inside from perspiration, outside from the rain. Everything harmonized to make things miserable.

There is no need of belaboring the fact that I started across the Yukon with twinges of trepidation. Luckily the dogs smelled home and were doing all in their power to get there quickly. On one occasion I went down to the tip of my hip boots and then simply hung on. The ice cake had tipped but the long string of speeding dogs had good footing, and were able to pull me out. I was within inches of an icy bath, if nothing worse. Nerves become jagged under such conditions. I began to see cracks where there were none, and dark spots where none existed. That kind of travel is the best cure for boredom that I know.

After eight hours of running, pushing, splashing, and wading (thank God there was no swimming except for the two dogs) I finally drew up near a small village. A huge V formation of Emperor geese flew high above me honking in the arrival of spring. My dogs dropped in their tracks on the muddy bank. There was no need to separate battlers this evening; they were too tired to remember old enmities. And I couldn't blame them much.

I walked into the cabin and found the people there more than a little concerned. Word of my coming had preceded me and when I didn't arrive within a reasonable time, they had visions of another of those springtime musher's accidents that continually take their toll. The smooth round face of the Eskimo can hide much of what goes on behind it, but occasionally they will let slip a word or two that indicates their concealed affection for their tramp missionary. That happened on this occasion, and did more than a little to warm and revive me after a trip that I would not like to tackle soon again.

I took my time over a steaming cup of tea. I could afford to relax a little now, because this was the last stop before home and I knew that the ice was better as I neared the Bering Sea. Even rain thaw wouldn't affect the trip which, with any luck at all, would take not more than a fast morning's mushing.

After Mass the next morning, my host cut my dogs each a juicy chunk of seal blubber. They wolfed it with smacking relish and then stood ready for the trail. The way these dogs can recover from the physical strain of a trip like that of the previous day is a constant source of wonder and admiration to me. They were beaten, and wet, and tired, and bleeding, and yet here they were eager and willing to start again on another day's work.

We started down the trail with a sober dash, but soon I could see the crimson trail appearing beneath me on the brittle ice. By this time even my spare dog moccasins had been worn out. So I could only follow and try not to notice. Finally even Berry, the "indefatigable," had to be unhooked from the lead and allowed to limp along behind us.

His stalwart son "Musso" took his place. The morning's travel stretched into the afternoon before weary dogs and a very weary musher staggered up the banks of the Mission. A long rest lay ahead; behind, there was a living baby and a dead woman both friends of God because of that extra little side trip. That gave the relaxation a certain zest it would not otherwise have had.

3. By Their Fruits...

IN THESE days of internationalism, the American people are apparently discovering for the first time one of their own more pronounced blindnesses. For so many years past we have thought consciously or unconsciously that we did things the right way, and everyone else was "outlandish." We drove on the right side of the street. We had the real way of greeting our friends. We acted properly in church. Everyone else was "queer."

But lately our soldiers have had the chance to see the customs in every corner of the world. They have had the further chance of meeting the people from those corners and found them "not really bad at all." So we are awakening gradually to the fundamental principle of internationalism, namely, that people can be different, and still be the same.

The Alaskan Eskimo is an outstanding example of that cultural difference. For years he has been accused by his white brethren of every kind of strange and unlovely habit. But for him who knows the Eskimo personality, all these differences fade into nothing more than an harmonious acceptance of a very different and a very difficult life.

The leisured habits of the Innuit are at first mistaken for laziness, but further acquaintance with the North and its stern ways soon convinces us that those habits are founded on a balanced sense of proportion and right living.

The Eskimo takes life as it comes and acts accordingly. He is so accustomed to meet the unexpected that the future, whatever it be, never causes him the least concern or worry. He is never in a hurry and for that reason he presses the most out of each minute of life as it passes.

The white man and his inventions for decimating time are to him a source of philosophic wonder. When you tell him with pride that you can cover in an hour by airplane a distance that would take him a week to cover with his dogs, he will only answer with a noncommittal grunt *"Eeee?"* (Yes?) — if you do not understand Innuit. If you know his language he will ask laconically, *"Chin?"* (Why, what's the rush?). To him, the impatient hustle of the white man is a puzzle. You inform him, quite readily, that it is to save time and he will ask why you want to save time.

Travel for him is not an interlude that must be gotten through. It is an integral part of his life, made especially enjoyable by stopping at every cabin or igloo on the trail. The traveling Eskimo is greeted everywhere with a hospitality that makes old-fashioned sociability look like hillbilly suspicion. He will drive up to a cabin on the trail with his seven or nine dogs, leisurely unharness them, enter the cabin without knocking, throw his reindeer skin on the floor and in general make himself pretty much at home. Whether he knows his host or not is no point for consideration. With the development of conversation, he is almost certain to find some common relation somewhere, a fourth cousin, maybe, and friendship is established.

The host supplies everything but sugar, a little tea, and a little flour. And his guest may stay a day, a week, or even a month, depending on his whim at the time. He simply moves into the family circle, and once in shares all its activities, such as catching fish, or cutting wood.

Concern for the future simply does not cross his mind. I have known an Eskimo to be weather-bound for weeks at a time. He simply takes it as a matter of course and with wonderful adaptability fits himself into his surroundings, whatever they may be. He knows better than to complain against the elements. His patience with things is so pronounced that a real swear word is not to be found in his whole language. The strongest Innuit expression is simply an emphatic "Pshaw!"

The white man with his incessant quarreling, complaining, swearing, money grabbing is a continual mystery to his limpid mind. He therefore calls his southern friend simply a "white." The word "man" is used exclusively in reference to the natives. When a white arrives in the North, the natives look placidly on, waiting to see how the stranger reacts to the impact of his stern motherland. He has seen many go down.

For, if anyone had a right to complain at his hard native lot, it is the Eskimo. His life is an everlasting shiver. He is tortured by the cold in winter, by the ubiquitous mosquito in the summer. His raiment is a tattered reindeer skin, his food merely tea and salmon with a little poorly cooked bread thrown in. In some districts he suffers a great deal from the dreaded tuberculosis. But he never complains, nor does he fear death. In his simplicity he wonders how the white man who has so much is so unhappy.

These fundamental Innuit qualities furnish a promising beginning for a real culture. For even in Eskimo land we can find development that will pass the test of true culture anywhere. A cultured native is not the product of those schools whose principal aim is to transform a native into a white. A cultured native is rather the finished specimen of the school which endeavors to bring out what is best in the native himself; which gives him an education based on an intelligent understanding both of the native mind and his natural environment. Such a man wins not only the respect of the whites, but he is honored by his own people as well.

On the other hand, the lot of the native who aspires to be a white is misery beyond misery. He is afflicted with a painful case of superiority complex whose foundation is a mystery to everyone but himself. He is too irresponsible to be a trusted employee of the whites. He is either too lazy or too conceited to stoop to fishing and trapping. His meager earnings are spent on the more lurid editions of white men's clothes. Unable to stand up against white competition in industrial or commercial enterprises, he gradually slips back to the life of the native for which he has been spoiled by contact with the whites. All in all his lot is a sorry one. The winter is spent in drifting from village to village, sponging off the working Eskimo who is too charitable to turn him away. His summer is taken up with odd jobs of longshoring or flunkying in miners' camps. His money is gambled away as fast as it comes, while his wiser brothers are storing food for the lean days of the winter.

And yet there is a rich store of human culture for the educator to work on in the native. The native is going back more and more, for example, to the richness of his own language. And it is well that he is, for it would be a crime to destroy his beautiful tongue. Innuit is rich beyond conception in structural variation. English would be a poor substitute for this great language. It would be a shaky vehicle to explain the refinements of description that the Innuit can effect. A native can describe the topography of the tundra, which to us is nothing but endless monotony, with a wealth of detail that would keep even a stranger from getting lost. And what is more, the native memory is so retentive that it can retain all this variety.

From a purely aesthetic point of view Innuit possesses a structural superiority to our language. Like the Greek, it used the dual form (to indicate the action of two people), and has a choice of moods impossible to translate into English. Unlike modern languages it is not forced to borrow words from foreign tongues. One root word will have as high as six hundred variations. A word is automatically fashioned to fit any modern invention. *Tingsoon* (the flying thing) came spontaneously to Eskimo lips when they first saw an airplane. So did *nichug'nissoon* (the thing that wants you to listen) at the sight of the radio; and *tanrstak* (that which makes you see) for the movie. In English my translation sounds clumsy, but in Innuit it is a perfectly descriptive term for the invention in question.

Let the educator therefore not destroy but rather preserve and cultivate the cultural advantages already inherent in the life of the native. Let him overcome the bad qualities that he will find, such as superstitions and a certain improvidence.

However, an intelligent understanding even of these faults in the native character is necessary. For instance, what is frequently called improvidence is nothing but the only way the native can react to his environment successfully. In his homeland the weather vane may swing to every point of the compass in the short space of twelve hours. Barometer needles play around like the hands of a clock. When a carefully planned trip goes awry and repeated delays pall on the active mind, the wise take it as a matter of course like the imperturbable Eskimo. Emergencies are best met, he finds from centuries of experience, by a saving sense of humor. However difficult it might be to find amusing details in a land of such grim possibilities, the Eskimo continually discovers them. He possesses a singularly simple and happy frame of mind, and can find a diversion in the most aggravating circumstances.

For instance, it is the easiest thing in the world to get lost on a bleak and barren tundra. A limitless sea of snow spreads out on all sides with only a straggling bush or a gentle rise in the ground to break the sameness. I have been lost only five miles

Kotzebue Church — The only one in the Arctic

Interior of St. Mary's Church at Akulurak

Igloo Church — Akulurak

Eskimo Huts — Kotzebue

Fr. O'Connor and Smaller Catechism Class — Kotzebue

Chicken in the Pot!

Tundra Eskimo Children

Akulurak Family and Grandchildren

Showing Off Baby

Adam and Eve

Lower Yukon Family

Solid Citizen

Akulurak Boy

Akulurak Family Drying Salmon

Cutting Salmon — Akulurak

from the Mission, and this with an experienced guide. It all
happened simply enough. A high tide forced us to make a short
detour. Deep snow and an unbroken trail delayed matters. In
less than an hour the sky was overcast and snow began to fall.
Before long we were completely befuddled in deep drifts and
impenetrable walls of hurtling snow. I had been on the trail for
some twelve days and wished to arrive at the Mission the following day which was Sunday. It was no use. Rather than sleep
out I backtracked on the trail for two more hours until I finally
reached a little trading post to spend the night. I was veary
and more than a little put out at being so close to home and
yet so far away. Not so my guide! He was chided by his friends
for missing the trail on such well-known ground, but he laughed
with them all and took it as a matter of course.

On another occasion I determined to have some fun with a
traveling companion. I was on a strange trail near the Kussilvak
Mountains. An old friend had kindly volunteered to show me
the way and incidentally make a little hunting trip out of it. The
two teams kept together all the way.

After a couple of hours on the trail we changed teams. I
noticed his rifle lying ready for use on the top of his sled. I
stopped his dogs and let my team drop out of sight in a little
creek bed. I hid the rifle inside his sleeping bag and a little later
caught up with him. We resumed the usual gossip of the trail
discussing the catch of fur, the palatableness of muskrat, and
so on. About an hour later a flock of ptarmigans was sighted
just off the trail. My Eskimo friend would not pass up a shot like
that. We immediately changed teams and he discovered the loss
of his rifle. He did not remember whether he had lost it or I.
He remarked with a smile that his gun must have bounced off
in some snowdrift.

The old adage about crying over spilt milk received a perfect application. He did not manifest the slightest impatience or mental disturbance. For the rest of the trip I kept up a steady flow of disparaging remarks about the loss of his gun. Not once was he touched by them. He had an answer to them all. The gun was old; he had a better one at home; he would fish for pike this trip instead of hunt. Finally he became concerned about my worry over the matter and silenced me by saying:

"Now, Father, don't you worry any more about that old gun. I have enough muskrats at home to buy three more like it."

This particular situation didn't ruffle the bland good humor of my friend for two very good reasons. First, if he had lost the gun himself, well, he would take care of that tomorrow. If I had lost it, well, everyone knows that the Eskimo is to share everything he has with others anyway, so why worry?

This law of sharing is universal among the Eskimos. In fact, a chief holds his authority over a village just as long as he is able to give. His influence is proportionate to his generosity. When this fails, his authority also will lessen and little by little pass to another. Conversely, a reputation for stinginess is probably the greatest curse that can fall on a family. To call an enemy *stingy* is to cap the climax of stinging epithets. To be stingy in the Arctic is the same as losing face in the Orient.

I have listened with amusement to endless arguments of an Eskimo trying to prove to another that he is not stingy. Nonetheless, I know for a certainty that I could wheedle anything out of a person if I were to insist opportunely enough that he was stingy. Rather than see me leave his igloo with this terrible conviction he would part with his last crumb of bread and his one remaining pinch of tea. Anything to prove that he was not stingy!

The most obvious result of this generosity is the Eskimo's love for a feast. At the slightest provocation he will declare a feast, and call his neighbors to share it. Has his fur catch been rich? He must feast over it. Has he been made happy by the birth of a grandson? He must have a feast — that, too, even in the lean winters when food is hard to come by.

And I must admit that all this "pans" out well in the long run. There is a regular round of feasting even during hard times. The poor and beggarly are just as welcome as the well-to-do. Their garments may be in tatters, their faces grimy, but the abdominal contours of the poor are just as round as that of their more successful brethren.

Here on the Yukon, for instance, if a whale is caught a feast is automatically declared for the entire village. Work is laid aside. Rich and poor, young and old, everyone is invited to have their fill, to partake of the feast. The whole community comes and rejoices. That lean and hungry days are ahead matters little or not at all. God will provide somehow or other for the future as He has provided for the past and the present. The feast at hand is worth two in the future. It doesn't matter that the whale was driven into shallow water by the genius and daring of a few mighty hunters. To save and hoard are unknown in this land of the perpetual iceboxes. Let all come to the feast, the hungry and the lazy indiscriminately. Even people from other villages are welcome; but they must be prompt, for the feast is to be had for the taking.

On another occasion a big brown bear may be killed by a brave and successful hunter. News of the killing spreads on a mysterious telegraph. All are welcome to come and feast. The hunter's house is crowded to the beams. Fat and bouncing Eskimo children crawl in somehow. Even *Agayulerta* (the Father) is not forgotten. A heart, or some other choice morsel is brought in triumph to his dwelling, and handed over with smiles enough to warm the Father's heart.

And as they feast, so they starve, without surprise and without question. I visited a little village close to the Bering Sea recently. Here all the huts are dugouts. They are completely buried in the snow with only the smokestacks peeking out. The man I stayed with had only caught one mink and one fox during the first month of winter. His larder was very low. Yet, he smilingly invited to supper all the young men who were attracted to his cabin by the presence of the priest. He gave out his last cup of tea with perfect and unwavering hospitality. He hardly remarked the disappearance of the last crumb of bread — the Father is here, take liberally of all I have. More will come somehow, sometime.

This was his calm and dignified attitude. It was immediately acted on without the slightest hesitation or embarrassment. I marveled how these young bucks went on imperturbably eating everything that remained in the house. The one food, black fish, would constitute the sole diet of that house for many a day to come. Nobody minded. This had often been done before. Maybe a fox would be caught or shot tomorrow. And the strangest thing about it all is that God usually takes care of these emergencies in that very manner. Certainly the Eskimo never worries about it.

Until I became accustomed to this complete trust and confidence in what the future would bring, it continually amazed me. But once I caught the spirit of the Eskimo, I began to see that it was just another of those cultural differences that keep men apart. Only this one is something beautiful, something warming, something very much to be desired in warmer lands where things are not always quite so difficult.

4. Akulurak

ONE of the unsolved mysteries of life is why people live on the Alaskan Tundra at all. It is one long, featureless expanse, a natural playground for roughneck windstorms. In winter it is a veritable ocean of snow and ice kept deceptively smooth by unobstructed gales. In summer it is a dreary swamp infested with billions of mosquitoes. There is no wood for protection or fuel and there is little food. But there is much fur, especially mink and muskrat, so I suppose that is at least part of the answer to the mystery of why one finds little villages of three or four igloos scattered all over the tundra.

Our mission at Akulurak is on the tundra of tundras. It occupies the highest ground on the lower Yukon delta. Father Treca, the apostle of the tundra, chose the site. This heroic old missionary spent more than a quarter of a century in this desolate region. Almost singlehanded he built St. Mary's Mission which is today the pride of the whole Alaskan mission. It must have taken the full power of the call of almighty God to bring him here. His family was rich and distinguished in the things of the world; in fact, it was due largely to their generosity that Father Treca succeeded so magnificently in doing what he did.

I had had a certain amount of experience with tundra dwellings, their low roofs, their cramped quarters, and their, shall we say, exotic odors. I knew that one could practically walk over a tundra village in the winter, and never even know it. I remembered the story of Father Delon having to make his camp at nine o'clock one evening. He knew he must be somewhere in the vicinity of the village he was headed for. He woke up the next morning and found the nearest house not ten feet away from where he slept!

So you can well imagine that I started on my initial trip to Akulurak, the heart of the tundra, with a little misgiving. I had heard of the glowing accounts of the Mission itself, but I had also seen enough of tundra life to make me qualify those accounts with what I chose to call "realism."

The two days I spent on the way were typical tundra days. A blizzard of soft snow made vision beyond the lead dog's nose impossible. The trail disappeared five minutes after starting. I couldn't help telling myself — "see, see what you are in for now, hero!" But on we pushed, me with my doubts, my guide with all the placid unconcern that the inscrutable Eskimo alone can display. After four hours on what might have been called a trail under happier circumstances, I asked my guide if he wanted a compass. He just grunted, twinkled a bit, and answered: "Me good compass."

How he found his way is another of those unsolved mysteries. But find it he did, without even a bush to guide him. On the second day about three-thirty in the afternoon I felt our sled slipping into a broad slough, and a few minutes later the blizzard parted enough for me to see five huge frame buildings. So here was Akulurak.

This Mission houses about one hundred children so you can imagine how large the two dormitories and the school had to be. It was only in the light of the following day that I had a chance to appreciate the size of the place. Here on this tundra rise was a wonderful set of buildings with every board and nail crying out the story of the unspeakable hardship and labor lavished on them by the earlier missionary Fathers and Brothers.

The remarkable thing about Akulurak, I was to find out, is that it is situated on a little knoll above the sweeping bareness of almost infinite snow. Not a tree in sight. On a clear day the eye can roam without let or hindrance as far as the Eskinok Mountains ninety miles away. The Mission itself has suffered two severe fires, and yet it stood before me that day, greater than ever, a fitting expression of the love and zeal that drives men to search out the least ones for Christ.

Many have doubted the advisability of maintaining a Mission like Akulurak. They speak of its expense, of the never ending labor entailed in keeping it up, of the backbreaking work of the Brother who every year must tow big rafts of logs sixty miles down the Yukon and then around 52 torturous turns of the Akulurak slough. They remind you that all freight must pass the same way. They speak obliquely of the boat trip down the slough, the drenching weather, the savage mosquito, the stink of Diesel fumes, and of a thousand other inconveniences involved in supplying this place.

But that is just the lower side of the tapestry. In spite of difficulties and discouragements, the work of our divine Lord cannot be measured in numbers, or in comfort, or in the usual meaning of the word "success." Some of the real significance of this Mission can be seen before any big feast day of the year, when upwards of sixty teams etch their dark lines across the snow, all leading to the Mission. It is a sight like this that makes one realize that all the labor has not been poured out unnoticed.

The first winter there I discovered that keeping warm was the prime concern at Akulurak. Stoking fires seemed to be our main occupation. And the cold refused to go. Rather late in the spring I woke up with the water frozen in my wash basin. Downstairs the water barrel, just four feet from the stove, frequently enough had a crust of ice on it. That was the end of

March, too! I could generally combat the cold by a mental warm-up over the indefinitely complex Innuit verb, but not always!

A frame house on the tundra offers an impossible problem of heating. I have caulked these mission buildings like a boat, and still, when that west wind opens up, the cold reaches through nonexistent cracks like ghostly fingers and searches to the bone.

One reason for that is the immediate location of the buildings. They are constructed over a glacier foundation. The result is that they move up and down with the advance and recession of the ice below them. Windows and doors are constantly jamming. New cracks and chinks are appearing puckishly from corners, and offering us plenty of ventilation. In the meantime the wood disappears as though some fire-eating giant breathed it in. Every missionary that has appeared on the scene sooner or later comes up with his theory on how to keep the buildings from their garish dance. But theories come and go, and the buildings keep moving up and down, up and down. And the cracks keep opening up. And the wood keeps disappearing. And the inhabitants keep shivering.

Our community amounts to one hundred, ninety of whom are orphan children gathered together from every corner of the tundra. To keep such an aggregation moderately warm fourteen stoves have to be kept going for eight or nine months of each arctic winter.

And this is how we do it.

After the smoke house is filled with fish and other necessary jobs are done, Brother Murphy and his crew of men and boys pile into the mission Diesel, and chug off in the search for wood. Forty miles and more of the broad Yukon is scoured for driftwood. Over mosquito-infested mud bars, logs are rolled and

fastened into rafts. Three weeks of deadening labor must be
spent before sufficient fuel is gathered together. The rafts are
then floated down the Yukon and around the fifty-two twisting
turns of the Akulurak slough. One has only to see this long
procession of rafts to realize the skill that directs their maneuvers
through a storm, and around the hairpin turns of the Akulurak.

Getting the wood to the Mission is only the beginning. Ten
days more are used in lifting the logs up the steep bank of
the mission grounds themselves. Then a buzz saw takes over
and everything up to fourteen inches is sawed into stove lengths.
During this period of sawing every man and boy in the Mission
is kept busy. All in all, a full month and a half of our precious
summer season is spent on the gathering of fuel alone.

It is work like this, especially the work of the selfless and often
heroic Jesuit Brothers that makes it possible to keep going at
all in some of these northern missions. If this wood were not
gathered, for instance, the cost of heating this plant alone would
be too much. But that is only one item. There are countless
other ways in which the expense of such an institution as this
is cut down to a figure that can be handled.

For one thing, our schools can be run on a third — even a fifth
of what it takes to run a similar government institution. Fortunately, and wisely, each mission is a complete unit in itself. The
Church, with all her so-called bureaucracy, has comparatively
little red tape tangling the efforts of individual members. The
absence of a monthly pay roll is a big item, of course. The mission superior does not receive a weighted check each month for
his services. Neither do the Brothers or teaching Sisters. They
are clothed and fed as superiors deem fit; they put off the
collection of all their pay checks to that final reckoning when
the check they will receive can never run out.

Missions also have a very real advantage over the public school up here in their permanent and steady teaching staff. Teaching religious come to Alaska with a fairly well-defined intention of adopting this work as their life. As a consequence, they settle down to making their work as fruitful and agreeable as possible. That is not always true of the public school teachers. Frequently enough they come to the North imbued with some of the rosy dreams I spoke of before, only to find that the first stretch of unrelieved winter is enough to dampen any ardors they might have had for the treasures of the Northland. Hence the frequent turnover in the teaching personnel. It is a little sad, incidentally, to think of the effect this has on the Eskimo pupil.

Careful planning and more careful preparation account for the rest of the saving. We have made our food staple from fish and potatoes, both of which we can take care of right here. Beyond that, flour, rice, and beans, with a little tea for extra, form the grand menu for the year. In terms of money this really isn't so much; in fact, five thousand dollars will carry this community of one hundred Eskimo children, the Fathers, Sisters, and Brothers through the whole year, including fuel, food, and oil. That is about $3.50 a month per person. It would be pretty hard to beat that for economy — and really, we are not so badly off, either.

Sometimes providence seems to take a huge delight in over-turning plan after plan, just to make us realize our dependence on God's help. For instance, my third year at Akulurak was something that made me realize God's providence is a very powerful force indeed.

The first in a long series of disappointments was the impossibility of putting in our usual garden. Snowdrifts in our yard lasted up to July 4. Ice jams at the mouth of the Lower Yukon prevented the usual abundant run of salmon. Our entire fishing season was disjointed, yet somehow we pulled out enough fish to feed both the children and our indispensable Malemutes during the winter. In spite of a noticeable absence of driftwood, Brother Murphy, at the cost of unbelievable labor, managed to snake down enough fuel for the omnivorous stoves.

Financial troubles and mismanagement found us just before the freeze-up without even the essentials of life. Our freight from the outside had been delayed, and then delayed some more, until the nerves of all concerned were jangling with worry and disappointment. I had met every boat up from the sea, all chuffing busily up the river with supplies for every place but Akulurak. We had been on limited rations for over a month. Even wine for Mass had to be cut down drastically. The prospect of facing a winter with one hundred orphan children eating nothing but fish began to make me feel old and very weary.

Then the word came up the river that the last boat was on its way. With death inside of me I went out to meet it. Winter was in the air. This had to be the one. Ice had already appeared on our water barrels. This had to be the one. The water in the Yukon was dropping steadily. This had to be the one. Sand bars poked sullen, vicious heads out of the water and blocked the usual channels. This had to be the one. It was only with anchors and winch that we were able to scrape over sand bars to reach the main river. This had to be the one. Then two yearlike days waiting on the Yukon. And then the steamer appeared around the bend. I don't think I breathed for a half hour. It finally moved in. It *was* the one!

The precious flour, rice, and beans for the Mission might have been so much mail from home for the joy they created in my heart. The steamer captain graciously loaned us one of his strong tugs to help us get back to the Mission with our loaded barges.

We left the river at once, for the water was dropping steadily. Just as darkness fell, a newly risen sand bar suddenly stopped the lead boat. The barge it was towing lumbered inevitably forward, and before we could draw a second breath, the towrope was hopelessly entangled in the propeller of the first. The next hour was heartbreaking — up to the waist in icy waters cutting the rope away from the strangled propeller. I marveled how my Eskimo boys could stand this freezing water for so long, and with such cheerfulness. This was to happen again the next day, in water still colder. At midnight with the benefit of a slight southerly wind we managed to scrape over the most dangerous spot. Eight times during that return trip it took every available ounce of power to keep the whole flotilla from being stranded. One inch less of water would have been fatal.

The next day, again with the wind at our backs, we succeeded in reaching home. An icy downpour of rain that trembled on the edge of being sleet did not dampen our cheerfulness as we rushed to unload, and free the river tug before the freeze-up. It left almost at once, but was caught in the running ice and had to return. The captain told me that another half hour driving against the razor-edged ice would have sunk the boat. It was doomed to winter here at the Mission, just ninety miles from home.

The very day after we unloaded, chill winds swept down from the north and froze the Akulurak River solid in one night. We had to chop the ice with our axes even to float our mission boats down to their dry docks.

When I had time to examine the freight I found that most of our necessary equipment had arrived. Some I had forgotten to order; that was made up by the gifts of thoughtful benefactors. Necessary clothing and medicines which I had ordered, but which had not arrived on this last boat, were supplied by other donations which I had no way of expecting. When the rush was over I spent a good long time in the church, adoring the inscrutable hand of providence that brings so much good out of so much apparent evil and disappointment.

It was that same year, late in the following spring, that Akulurak Mission picked up the modest little job of supplying all the neighboring missions with enough salmon for men and dogs! This is how it happened.

Our fishing season that year began earlier than usual (as though to make up for the poor one the year before). Salmon were running by the thousands. In the midst of the whirling excitement and fever of concentration, I heard from Reverend Father Provincial himself, by radio telephone, that he would be down the river from Holy Cross in a few days. We were caught flat-footed. House not painted; floors unscrubbed; the smell and grime of fish everywhere. Well, anyway, the boss would get a chance to see how Akulurak could fish.

A few days later about midnight I was awakened by a strange chug on the river. I slipped into my clothes and noticed, not without a certain perverse satisfaction, that the mosquitoes were riding abroad in waves. I greeted Father Provincial at the boat landing, and we fought our way through clouds of bloodthirsty drillers up to the house. When Father asked me if the mosquitoes were always this bad, I looked around innocently and asked in turn, "What mosquitoes?"

Fr. Joseph McEmeel, the superior of the Alaskan Mission, arrived unexpectedly the next day. Then came Fr. Endal from Mountain Village; Fathers Fox and Deschout from Hooper Bay and Nelson Island respectively. We isolated Akulurakateers, who are lucky to see one strange white face a year, stood aghast at this inundation of visitors. Conventions and all that are very fine. I like conventions. But the sight of this gang of lean and hungry missionaries made me mentally kiss my provisions goodby. I cautioned Sister cook, in front of my visitors, of course, to be very careful! Luckily for me, the salmon were running. I suggested, with all the enthusiasm of a Waldorf chef that we have salmon, done in three most interesting ways. It is so intriguing, don't you know.

We had salmon. In fact we had salmon both living and dead. For it wasn't long before these men of the open North decided that they should know more about handling a fish run. So we had some help on the fish run.

Fr. Endal donned hip boots and stepped up to the cutting machine to show expert talent at snapping the heads from the incoming fish. In the meantime, of course, he had tactfully suggested to Brother Feltes, my engineer, that his boat needed overhauling and a reverse gear.

Frs. Fox and Deschout volunteered with suspicious alacrity to bundle fish. I stood by in admiring silence and watched their surprising efficiency, exactly forty pounds to a bundle. Their industry did not cease until the bundles themselves were again loaded into their own boat, to the accompaniment of bland smiles and soft words of untold gratitude. All I could do was smile back, toss my hands in the air, and blow away my dreams of bettering the financial status of Akulurak by disposing of surplus fish!

And that is how this Mission got the job of supplying dried fish to all the neighboring missions. As we drew up the plans for this transaction I thought to myself, rather happy now after the thing had been accomplished, that a brother helped by a brother is actually like a strong city after all. It was a wonderful thing that St. Mary's Mission, besides helping the natives that clustered around her, could send her help farther and farther into that field where Christ walks, gathering sheaves for His granaries.

5. Easter Invitation

ALL through the last chapter I had a lot to say about the Mission of Akulurak, about its finances, and location, and difficulties. But it was all from the inside out, as it were. This time I would like to have you come and pay me a visit. And, since visits up here are something of an occasion, it might be well to pick the time of a big celebration. Easter will do. I'm sure that you will see many things during an Easter celebration up here that will make your visit well worth your while.

Be sure to follow directions on your trip up. You can get boat passage at this time of the year up to Seward, Alaska. A train will then drop you off at Anchorage. From there a plane with skis will pick you up and carry you over a vast, white region of which there seems to be no end. Six or seven hours' flying time ought to bring you to the Yukon. The plane will circle, and swoop down to some little village on the lower fork of the river. Here, since Akulurak is a little outside the circle of usual travel, I will volunteer to pick you up by dog team.

The plane has stopped rolling. The flyer is a little anxious, for blizzards and foul weather can sweep in at a moment's notice and make his flight back something you wouldn't bet on with any sense of security. He doesn't kill his engine; only chokes it down a little. Then he is off, into the gray skies of the south. You look rather skeptically at my dogs. There are eleven of them there, and they are looking you over with that indefinable superiority which only an Alaskan husky can convey. You will certainly notice that they are different from dogs that you have

38

known before. They have big heads and chests; they need them for the work that lies ahead. They are lean and hard from the two thousand miles of travel during the past winter. When we walk over to the sled, they leap up and strain at the harness, literally rarin' to go. It is a good thing that the anchor rope is holding them fast.

After I have seated you comfortably in the sled, I loosen my towline, and away we go.

It isn't long before I notice you blinking your eyes at the glare of the sun on the snow. You are beginning to understand now why the Eskimo is almost invariably squinting. I have made it a point to carry two pairs of snow glasses with me. So now I give you one, and put the other on myself. With the strain of the sun's brilliant glare relieved, you relax. But after a few more hours on the trail, you begin to feel your face burning. And it is, for the sun comes now from below, reflected from the snow beneath you.

We pass several teams on the trail. Now that your experience has awakened you, you notice that every musher we pass is masked with goggles and a face almost black from sun-snow burn. And then I have to tell you about the danger of passing another team on a soft trail. Unless the leader is smart and well trained the ensuing dogfight can very well be almost disastrous. But today, thank God, the surface is hard, and it is no trick at all to give each oncoming team a wide berth by turning off the trail into the snow beside it.

If I were to recount to you at this stage of the game the number of dogfights that I had to settle with a "black snake" you would probably be a lot more uneasy than you are. Berry, my leader, the one that holds himself so proudly there, and answers so quickly and unerringly my shouted commands, likes nothing better than a good free-for-all. The two long-legged swing dogs, Banjo and Monkey, are as gentle as lambs and good friends with the leader. But behind them is Sax, another fighter who longs to settle an old account with Berry. Sax, however, is perfectly contented as long as Scotty, a lively and handsome youngster, travels at his side. These dogs are a good deal like naughty little boys. They have strong likes and dislikes. Their interest centers mainly around their stomachs, but if there is any trouble around, they are bound to get into it. But they forget a scolding or a whipping with the same eager wagging that you see in a reprimanded child. They are lovable beasts, interesting beasts, and almost insanely jealous of the affection of their master. I guess that is why I love them so.

By now we have left the Yukon and are swinging south by compass. Akulurak is about forty miles ahead into the isolation of the Alaskan tundra. This isolation, by the way, is not a complete curse. It helps one to carry on his missionary activity unimpeded by malicious white influence. The problem of the half-breed, for instance, has not yet arisen at Akulurak, for there is nothing there to attract white adventurers. There are no mines on the tundra. The mosquitoes and weather are enough to keep most sight-seers away. The winds themselves, biting and penetrating and damp from the Bering Sea, have taken a heavy toll already from the ranks of the Jesuit missionaries and the Ursuline Sisters.

We stop on a little rise for lunch. A sip of coffee from a thermos bottle and a sandwich. Please don't worry about this meager lunch; it will make you appreciate all the more the delicious reindeer roastette which the Brother at the Mission is even now preparing for your arrival. The dogs are rolling in the snow and taking their needed rest. Off in the distance we can see the mirage of the Mission buildings. The church is magnified into the grand proportions of a cathedral. You think they are quite close, but actually it will take another three hours of fast travel to get there.

We feed the dogs. They know they are approaching home, and it is a task to keep them still long enough to get ready for our start. Finally we cast off again, and away we go with increasing speed as we approach the buildings ahead. As we draw near you can see the stately church, a modest school building, and a house for the sixty girls and five Ursuline Sisters. Over there beyond the church is the Fathers' house which also is the home for over thirty Eskimo boys. You will notice that there is nothing lavish about these buildings; they are strong, solid, pre-eminently practical.

The Mission itself is teeming with life and action, quite a contrast to the solemn stillness of the trail that some mushers find almost appalling. Here, however, the cheery voices of the Eskimos come from every side. You begin to hear sounds that you never thought could come from the mouth of man. That is the Innuit language. After about one thousand hours of study, I have almost concluded that the language is in the same class with the mosquito, the more you fight it, the worse it is.

Later from your window you look out on at least a hundred dogs tied to the willows on the opposite bank of the Akulurak slough. They are snapping at their chains, baring their teeth at loose dogs, and setting up an internal din which you think you will never get used to. For your comfort, I remind you that you are looking at only about a quarter of the dogs that will be here for the celebration. My own grim Malemutes watch with obvious distrust this intrusion of so many strange dogs into their domain. Oddly enough, in spite of all the sound effects, there are few dogfights, and no dead dogs.

Then Holy Saturday dawns. We go through the long, solemn ceremonies, and you notice with interest that there is not a moment of flagging attention on the part of my Eskimos. They can't read, most of them, but their watchful scrutiny misses nothing. The blessing of fire, of the Paschal Candle, the Baptismal Water, everything is taken in with rapt and solemn interest.

After it is over, you can accompany me, if you wish, as I bless each house in the village, a time-honored Holy Saturday custom. The cabins are all full to the brim with visitors. Your nose, I know, will be wrinkled by sudden and violent odors such as seal oil, or *Akutak* (Eskimo ice cream), but withal, you can't help noticing the general air of neat contentment and simple comfort.

Then at noon we return to the church, packed now with the fur-clad Eskimos. No bashfulness about their singing. The church rocks to the alternate refrains of the *Regina Coeli Laetare*. You are beginning to see the fruits of the Ursulines' work, reaching now to the third generation.

Then in the afternoon I will leave you free while I hear confessions. You might drop over to the Sisters' house to take a look at the girls' work. You will see needlework of such exquisite taste and precision that you will hardly believe it came from these solemn little ladies of the North. Another gift from the Ursulines to the native here. This evening we will watch a hockey game on the hard snow just behind the Mission. It will be fought to the finish, and you will probably see several of the older Eskimos leap into the fray before it is over.

Then Easter dawns, as Easter should, in dazzling brilliance. At the Communion Mass you can see the church packed with over four hundred Eskimos. Almost all have come by dog team. Every woman has a baby strenuously demanding attention. The men for the most part have taken off their parkas as they enter the church. The women though, have combined every possible color in their calico overparkas. They wear silk scarves of brilliant hues over their heads. The altar is massed with artificial flowers, the work of the skillful hands of the blushing Innuit maidens. Then the priest begins the Mass and is answered in Latin by the entire student body of the school. Easter hymns both in English and Innuit swell up periodically during the Mass.

Then the high Mass, at nine-thirty. Again the church is packed. The congregation sings the ancient Gregorian Mass with such precision and feeling that you begin to wonder if you are listening to the monks of Solemnes. Most of these Innuits do not read, but their facile and retentive memories make learning the Latin ceremony a thing of relative ease. You are surprised I know, to see the entire congregation go through the whole Mass without aid of missal or prayer book. These are not passive worshipers waiting for the whole thing to end. They are a part of the sacrifice, the articulate Body of Christ, giving expression to the longing of the Church in exile through the beautiful liturgical prayers of love, adoration, and petition.

And then the sermon. In spite of my grim efforts with the language, I still must use an interpreter. And a hard job he has, too, because of the simple, concrete nature of his own language. I have found that a straight retelling of the parables of the Gospel, or a brief little talk on one simple idea serves best. Abstractions are out completely.

After the Mass there is no rushing and scrambling to leave the church. The Eskimo does not hurry life, hence does not hurry his prayer life. He makes the most of the richness of each present moment. The future will be taken care of when it comes. I doubt, in fact, if their simple, concrete minds can even picture the future as something which must be reckoned with.

After lunch we will walk over to the boat shed to look at the new launch we have just finished building. There is a long story behind that boat. For the past thirty years St. Mary's Mission has experimented with all kinds of boats. Some are good for speed, some for power; some are good for shallow water, some only for the deeper draft. We have never before been able to combine all these features in one boat.

For over two years Father Anable, Brother Murphy, and Brother Feltes planned and drafted. Finally they came up with a model that seemed to fit each need. It had to be sturdy enough to stand the sand-bar work of the Akulurak slough; fast enough to bring the fish in the forty-five miles from the traps before they spoiled; powerful enough to swing huge log rafts around those killing turns in the Akulurak; and big enough to handle untold freight from the Yukon itself.

After checking the final plans with some boat architects in Seattle we sent in our order. You can imagine how detailed that order had to be, down to the last nut and bolt. With some old scrap iron, an acetylene torch, and a lathe, plus the genius of Brothers Murphy and Feltes, we began the work. As needs cropped up we broadcast them over our radio, and soon the whole Seward peninsula was covered with a network of willing helpers. Once we had to send a dog team on a three hundred mile round trip to pick up some material that didn't get on the incoming freight boat. All through the long winter the men worked, helped by some expert Eskimo carpenters, graduates of the school here.

Little by little our boat took shape. As spring drew to an end and summer began we had as high as twenty men working on the boat at once. Many of these fellows had deliberately passed up their more lucrative muskrat hunt just to be sure that the boat would be ready for the fishing season. To the amazement of the skeptical old Yukon boatmen, we finally slid her down the

ways in record time. We solemnly christened her the *Sifton,* after
a grand old missionary who had done so much for Alaska.

We had launched it just in time for the beginning of the
fishing season, so the *Sifton's* shakedown cruise was one of strict
business. Up to the fishing camp we purred at 1500 revolutions
a minute, not at a mere seven and a half miles an hour against
the current which had been predicted, but at a full ten. The
counterbalanced rudder and prop worked like a charm, lifting
easily over hidden sand bars without the slightest hitch. We
actually went over eighteen inches of water without hesitation.
On the other extreme, we have since gone out into the Bering
Sea and weathered huge rollers sweeping down from the Arctic.
You can well see why we are proud of this cruiser of ours,
especially since it was built for about one third of what it would
have cost under any other circumstances.

It's really too bad I cannot take you for a little ride, but the
ice is no respecter of persons. Anyway, we must visit the Sisters'
house. There are several of those heroic ladies I would like to
have you meet before you go.

You know, it is easy to write about the difficulties and hardships of the missionary on a blizzardy trail. There is always the
thrill of movement, of seeing a long string of beautiful dogs
leading out into the whiteness ahead. But there is little romance
and less thrill in mending endless *mukluks,* or darning innumerable socks, or washing children's clothes, and handling soggy
overalls — all in subzero weather through the long months of
the Arctic winter. And yet all this disheartening work is done
repeatedly, sometimes even daily by these nuns you will meet
over there; often with a song and a quick little laugh that supplies sunshine for the dark winter days.

Serving and eating seal oil (always obnoxious to the smelling instincts of the white), or baking infinite loaves of bread only to see them disappear as if by magic down the hungry throats of a hundred children. Then to move from the bakery out into the snow, when the difference in temperature is often as much as 120 degrees — it is a wonder to me how these delicate American women of God can stand the strain of such a difficult life. The daily teaching in the schools crowded with natives who at best only tolerate school — all this will demand almost the fullness of heaven itself to repay it adequately.

And yet the Ursuline Sisters, and the Sisters of St. Ann go through their endless days with placid dignity and charm, filling out with each day's work all the infinite little details of a life full of unexpected beauty. There is no hundredfold here, except perhaps in the warm confidence shown by the students old and young. Frequently these young men and women, perhaps five years away from the school, will travel all day to visit one or more of their religious teachers, just to impart a confidence, or get advice, or encouragement. In this manner the Sisters labor in every one of the Alaskan missions. Thus it is that five Ursuline nuns keep one hundred children fed, clothed, and educated here at Akulurak.

On almost every trip the missionary makes, he brings home some little ragamuffin off the tundra. This little boy or girl comes wide-eyed into the Mission, speaking not a word of English. Their dress, especially if they be orphaned, as most of them are, is the shabbiest, and filthiest. The sisters receive this unpromising subject with the kindly, businesslike bustle of long experience. A systematic scrubbing reveals the fresh young skin of the surprised little native. Hair is clipped or bobbed, clean clothes provided. Then almost before your eyes the transformation takes place. Prayers are learned in both English and Innuit. School begins, with its emphasis on the skills and crafts that will best fit the child to take his place in the native surroundings he will later encounter. To appreciate what these Sisters have done with the children you see around you, you should see the original product. It is just short of miraculous.

It is true that these Ursuline nuns never come into much immediate contact with the impressive fruit of their labors. Yet I do. Out on the trail I am constantly walking into a cabin or igloo of a former pupil. Immediately I notice the difference; a deep, friendly respect for me as a priest; an added cleanliness and order around the place; indications of artistic interest in carvings and needlework. Then night prayers are said with a precision and interest that indicates long practice. Mass is heard with intelligent intention.

I have countless times said to myself as I left a place like that, that God must be very pleased with this selfless, sacrificial work that the Sisters do for these forgotten natives of His. I would like to be around for the welcome these ladies will get when they go home for the rest they have denied themselves during long years of devoted service of their Lord in the northern wastes.

6. Home Sweet "Igloo"

THE time of the Equinox in Alaska is one of turbulent weather changes, from bitter arctic cold to warm winds, and blizzards of huge flaky snow. The trail during this season can be glassy smooth, or as sticky as wet dough. On the former the musher exults like a giant to run his course; on the latter, well, the less said the better.

Through all of March I watched these wayward and lightning-like changes of weather. It was impossible to travel except for occasional rabbit drives or to visit tundra villages in the immediate vicinity of the Mission. Needless to say, I missed the crisp days of February with their cold freshness and the star-spangled nights ribboned with flashes of northern lights. Even bad weather finally ends, though; and I thought that after a month the winds had played enough tag on this desolate coast of the Bering Sea. Anyway, I had to visit my scattered flock and give them a chance to make their Easter duties. I was to find out that the first of April is not called the feast of fools without reason.

I left the Mission in a dense fog. It was fairly cold. Soon the fog frosted our parkas, eyebrows, and eyelashes, and transformed my Malemutes into huge silver foxes. In spite of a good pace over the hard trail, I was soon overtaken by three native mushers on their way to a seal hunt. To one sled was strapped a kayak for the open sea. As much as I would have enjoyed accompanying them, I had to satisfy myself with the fact that we were to be together for about fourteen miles. Dogs like company as well as man, and always go faster when they have the scent of other dogs ahead of them. This was to prove the undoing of one poor half-starved Siberian later on.

We had covered about eight miles when all of a sudden my dogs caught a scent, probably of a fox, and off we galloped in the fog. I heard shouts behind me but thought for a moment that my friends, the seal hunters, were simply urging their dogs on to greater speed. Through the hubbub, however, I heard the word *Agayulerta!* (Father!) and immediately halted my team. *Naskopak* (Bighead) soon appeared standing on a brake that did not hold. His dogs were racing to catch my team, but one wheel dog had fouled his harness and had been dragged several hundred yards by the neck. My boy grabbed the leader and halted the team. The pure white Siberian was bleeding at the mouth and apparently lifeless. His harness was gingerly unfastened (these animals are vicious when they are in pain), he was then flung unceremoniously on the sled and our journey was resumed.

As we neared the Bering Sea the fog became denser. This we did not mind, for the trail was easy to follow. And if the fog melted we would have the sun and a very soft trail in consequence. Before long my Eskimo friends turned off sharply to the sea. I kept on alone. Not a sound except the soft patter of dogs' feet, the swinging of the harness, and the silence itself, so deep that one could actually hear it. Just ahead of me rose up a big mound of snow. It was a single igloo.

Permit me to explain for a moment the usual dwelling of the Eskimo away from the more populated area of the Yukon banks. The house frame consists of logs or old boards gathered from anywhere and everywhere. These rude timbers are braced and arched, and mud blocks are thrown over them. As a rule they are not above six feet high in the center. The floor is either the earth itself or a few rough boards. The entrance is a little tunnel made out of ice blocks. There is a lone window, generally on the south side of the slanting roof. It is sometimes of glass, more often of seal or whale gut. The amount of light that can get through such a skylight arrangement is quite surprising.

In soft weather the igloo is a miserable, damp place in which to live. I have been in several when it was necessary to erect the summer tent inside the igloo to keep the bed clothing from getting soaked. Igloos are at their best in very cold weather, especially when a northern blast is raging over the tundra. For then they are completely covered beneath the snow, are airtight and require very little fuel to heat them. Ventilation, of course, is out of the question. Nor is sanitation a matter of glossy linoleum, gleaming tile, and glittering chrome.

Still, I have often remarked that an Eskimo is much cleaner, fresher looking, far more careful of clothing and footwear than a white flung into the same conditions for any length of time. I must confess that I feel nothing but an amused impatience for those whites who come to Alaska for a year and then write voluminously about the habits of a people whose language and psychology of life they have scarcely begun to understand. Invariably they speak of the filth of the Eskimo. Let them look around and see for themselves how whites, transplanted into the same conditions, have fared in that perpetual war with the elements which is the miserable lot of the tundra Eskimo.

The barking of the dogs is the only sign of a stranger's approach that these igloo dwellers have. As I drew near, the dogs barked and the inmates popped out at once.

Our greeting was a usual one in my "parish"; wide grins, the quick crackling of hearty well-wishing, and a warm invitation to come in. So I crawled through the entrance tunnel.

Water was dripping from the ice blocks. You see, the day was beginning to warm up. I stepped down into the lowly habitation of one of the Mission's first school girls — Lucy. I looked around, and was warm and glad to see that her house was clean and that her children were well booted. I can judge at once a youngster's mother simply by looking at his sealskin boots. A good mother, though she has seven or eight children, has them all well shod.

I talked with Lucy first. I asked her about herself, her family, the past winter. But all the while I was searching her face (without seeming to look at all) for those indefinable signs which reveal so much, even in the wide and placidly friendly countenance of the Eskimo. It is not good for a missionary to miss those signs, for he can be of great help if he is sharp enough to read what it is that the Eskimo wants him to talk about. And especially in the case of that shy lady of the far snows, the Eskimo woman.

For the part an Eskimo woman plays in life is hardly one of liberal emancipation. Life in this stern northland is hard at best. It is not surprising, therefore, that few women pass the half-century mark. The few that survive receive the name of *Mauhulok* — "Old Granny." Having weathered a life of subjection and hardship she now begins to rule, and rule she does with an iron hand. I have learned from experience to respect these ancient dames. In conflict with them the wise proceed with caution. Diplomacy becomes the *modus procedendi.*

Let me explain in detail just what Grandma has to pass through to win her exalted position. It is not mere chance or blind custom that raises her to a level equal to that of the village chief himself. As a matter of fact, frequently enough the village chief has to take dictation from a very irate, or very determined *grande dame.*

Usually, it is not long after nature proclaims a maiden to be a woman that her hand is asked and given in marriage. The bride has little to say about the choice of her partner in life. Parents or guardians follow the Asiatic custom and consider themselves quite capable of judging the eligibility of her husband. They have more facts at hand to evaluate a husband than has the young lady. Romance as we understand it gives way to a cool and dispassionate evaluation of the Eskimo couple's compatibility. I might add, also, that the percentage of happy marriages resulting from this type of matchmaking is far higher than that of our romantic marriages in the States.

Children, of course, are the stabilizing element in matrimony. The desire for children once in a while becomes almost ruthless. A barren woman will be abandoned sometimes in favor of one that is productive. Adoption of children, however, is the more frequent solution. I have seen mothers give away a baby to a lonely couple with absolutely no expression of sentiment. The answer invariably is — "I have three children, they have none. I am not stingy." Life in an igloo without the sunshine of children is considered no life at all. Children are the wealth and happiness of an Eskimo home. Without them the igloo is merely a dugout, not a home.

The married woman on entering her husband's mansion finds a floor with or without the luxury of boards. The dugout will measure some twelve by fourteen feet. In my tundra district here on the Yukon Delta not more than five families out of a hundred have two-room houses. The bed will be simply a raised platform covered with a reindeer mattress. A rabbit-skin covering will probably be the only blanket. This rude bunk takes the place of a chair and lounge during the day. Eskimos are not averse to sitting on the floor. Often, for instance, when they come to visit me they will refuse a comfortable chair, to squat Chinese style on the floor. The native hut will also contain a tiny stove, the top of which hardly measures more than eighteen inches square. It is an inevitable anxiety to see a tea kettle, a pot full of boiling fish, and a five-gallon can filled with thawing ice piled precariously on such a surface. For dining purposes there is a miniature table, six inches high, which can be conveniently hidden underneath the bed during off hours (which are not so many, incidentally). Boots, parkas, mittens, guns, drying frames for skins, and innumerable other tools of northern life will be hanging from every available inch of wall and ceiling. No space is lost in these lowly dugouts.

It does not take long for our bashful Eskimo bride to put her house in order. Her work begins at once. She must go down to the creek or lake and chop ice. Over on the Yukon there are water holes — not so on the tundra. Here ice is very thick. Creek beds will often be frozen to their very bottom. With a practiced stroke of her ice pick or ax she soon fills two five-gallon oilcans with ice and heaves them up a slippery bank. The arduous task of providing water is a daily chore no matter how inclement the weather. It is probably providential, however, since it forces the women away from the fetid atmosphere of the igloo into the cleansing freshness of the outside air at least once a day.

Cooking is not such a difficult task. Fish or reindeer are invariably boiled. No condiments at all are used. Salt may be added during the meal to suit the individual taste. Seal oil is also at hand to be used as a sort of dressing. Bread is not taken during the meal proper. It is eaten at the end, when tea is served. The Eskimo drinks his steaming tea with noisy efficiency from a saucer. It is taken with or without sugar, according to the finances of the house at the time. When lard is available, it is used like butter, and considered quite a luxury. Reindeer fat is the usual grease for baking bread.

It is clear, then, that cooking is not much of a problem for the housewife. In the morning a pot of fish is put on the stove.

It simmers all day and may be taken whenever the family feels hungry. The principal meal of the day is served in the evening when the husband comes from his traps. After that, frozen raw fish is given as a lunch just before bed. Pike, tomcod, greyling, or blackfish, frozen solid, are cut up and eaten with great gusto. I have often marveled how and where the short stocky Eskimo can put away all he eats. Constant exercise in cold weather seems to provide limitless gastronomic capacity.

As difficult as some of these domestic elements might seem, I personally think that sewing is the most tedious occupation in the Eskimo domicile. Both men and women are expert with the needle. Naturally, of course, it is the more usual work of the housewife. Their stitches made with reindeer sinew are of such precision and finesse that a *mukluk* (outside boot) is both airtight and waterproof. To keep a family of five or six perpetual-motion machines well shod is an endless and heroic task. The soles, especially of children's boots, require constant attention. The smallest tear will let in cold air or freezing water. As you know, feet need exceptional care in a cold, wet climate. Eskimo mothers instinctively know this, and are thus ever on the alert. I might remark in passing that the quality of a woman's stitch is noticed much more quickly than that of her physical charms. Men up here unconsciously note the one and pass up the other. When they are in search of a wife their manner of expression is . . . "I have no one to sew my boots."

I have found the Eskimo boot, or *mukluk*, the warmest, lightest, and in general the most comfortable footgear that I have ever used. Unfortunately it requires the everlasting attention of a woman, as I remarked before. On the trail, therefore, I invariably hand my traveling *mukluks* to the woman of the house for inspection and reshaping. Incidentally, one changes his *mukluks* respectively from one foot to the other every day to preserve their shape. There is no such thing as a left or right *mukluk*.

Not many American women, I presume, would change places with her lowly Innuit sister. I might remark, however, that the lady clothed in fur has no worries, no wrinkles, no nervous disorders with their consequent tonics and pills, no gray hairs until they are properly becoming. In spite of her life of hardship and cold, she is happy and contented. Then, too, together with all the daughters of Eve, she has her smart set of furs for gala occasions, and (need I add) her irrepressible flow of gossip.

But enough of that — back to my host and hostess.

Inside the igloo I found a visitor to the house whose baby had not been baptized. A few more moments and this bland-faced little pagan had become a wet-faced, wrinkling little Christian. The father of the family was anxious to get off for a seal hunt; I, too, wished to reach the next village before the sun moved too high over the horizon. So we each used the other as a graceful excuse for departure.

On the trail soft weather again enveloped us. I needed neither parka nor beaver cap, but I did need my sunglasses. They were now of prime necessity to keep me from going blind in the terrific glare of the sun on immaculate snow. The sled sank. The trail was heavy and sticky. Gone now was the thrill of mushing; gone, too, was the romantic, majestic North. Instead, enervating heat deadened our spirits, dulled our senses. The dogs no longer sprang with elastic step over the trail. Their tails drooped. The heavily furred brutes dragged and gasped, and perspired freely through their mouths. Time and again my brave huskies looked over their shoulders pleadingly as if to say — "Come on, chum, let's call it a day and dig in for a cool little snooze."

I am happy to be able to say that during over ten years

of steady mushing I have never yet killed a dog on the trail. I take a certain pride in caring well for these faithful animals. Even on my long trips to Kuskokwim from Holy Cross, which sometimes took twenty-one days, I came back with the tail of every dog waving in the air; they were hardened by steady work, but not exhausted.

A couple of more hard miles and we were at Kanyak. It is impossible to sneak up and surprise a village no matter how deeply the snow has buried it. The advance notice of barking dogs brought all the kids scurrying out of their white retreats and plowing through the heavy snow to give me a greeting full of smiles and snapping eyes.

7. Eskimo Children

I HAD already determined to spend the night here, not only to rest the dogs but also to give several old Mission children a chance to approach the sacraments. While the boys were unhitching my dogs I made a hasty tour of the village. In one igloo I found a mother skinning a seal. The igloo itself was small and parts of the seal were lying everywhere. There was hardly room here to stand, much less to lay me down to sleep. I stood there marveling at the dexterity of three tiny Eskimo girls who were helping their mother in the dismemberment of the seal. Blood was all over their hands and clothes, but they didn't mind. In fact, they were bubbling over with enthusiasm for a task that was even then making me smile yellowly, and turn instinctively to the freshness of the outside.

I floundered along a few yards, then stooped along the passageway of a neighboring igloo. In this one, besides the parents, there were five wriggling children in very narrow quarters. One new arrival put up a strong protest against my coming. No, there was certainly no room for me in this inn. But before I left, I passed a few pleasant words with papa and mamma, in the meantime grinning at the lively antics of the five children.

What was true here was true everywhere among the Eskimos. He may lack the material comforts of life, but he is rich in children. For, if the peculiar effect of riches is to bring pleasure and prestige, then the Eskimo father and mother consider themselves millionaires if their igloo is filled to overflowing with bouncing babies.

The Eskimo's philosophy of life is much less selfish than the average birth controller. Since he is not swamped with modern luxuries, his vision is not blinded by them. Material comforts are in one category; children in another, like size and wisdom. He would not think of weighing them on the same scale at all. He judges that physical convenience is, after all, a certain accident of life, and at times can be sacrificed: But a baby! Why, that is life itself! The desire for children has occasionally led to its own lawlessness. Experimental unions in isolated districts of the tundra are even yet contracted with the sole purpose of determining the fertility of a prospective wife.

Babies therefore are riches beyond riches. Both parents are one in this conviction. Even health and sickness are minor considerations in the production of life. Life itself — life expressed in babies, is what counts. It is probably because the Eskimo has to fight so earnestly to conserve life that he values its production. I have known mothers afflicted with chronic ailments which make childbirth an act of heroism, yet they did not falter or make excuses. To thwart birth or conception does not cross the horizon of their imagination. A woman would feel nothing but shame and sadness if she were simply a wife and not a mother.

As a consequence, babies abound in Alaska. They are coming all the time. Almost every trip with my dogs I find two or three ready for baptism. I have about two hundred families in my tundra parish, scattered in tiny villages within a hundred-mile square. You will be surprised to hear that my baptismal records average between forty and fifty babies a year.

Personally, I find that the administration of baptism is one of the most consoling functions of the priesthood. I will go a long way off the trail to baptize a baby Eskimo, the news of whose birth has been relayed to me by *Mukluk telegraph.* For there is a high rate of infant mortality in this severe land of bare survival.

I have often wondered in the long, silent moments on the trail what a large assembly of little Eskimo angels must have lined up in singing welcome for the souls of the veteran Alaskan missionaries as they mushed into their last golden village of all desires. How many thousands must they have baptized in their long career of thirty and forty years of continual ministry!

With so many baptisms each year, names become quite a problem. Lately I have been naming the boys after the doctors of the Church; the girls, on account of their multiplicity, must be satisfied with the names of martyrs. After all, their lot in life will not be an easy one, so why not give them appropriate patron saints?

In conferring names one must proceed with utmost caution. Let me exemplify. One day last summer the Mission boat was chugging past one of the fish camps along the Yukon when suddenly a kayak shot out. The priest slowed down.

"*Agayulerta,* I gotta baby. You baptize him."

"By all means," replied the priest. "When did he come?"

"He come — mebbe five days, mebbe six — he want baptism."

Before long the priest had his kit laid out in the little tent and was ready to proceed with the wriggling infant.

"How about 'Paul' for a name?" he asked.

"No."

"Peter?"

"No."

The priest rapidly went over a dozen names; an emphatic "no" met each one. The saints of the Society of Jesus received scant consideration, not to say scorn. Finally, in despair, the priest curtly asked,

"Well, what name do you want, anyway?"

"Fadder, my baby, he's a girl!"

I said my *adieu* to the whole family, parceled out a few pieces of hard candy to the eager kids, and left.

My next igloo was a two-roomed affair. In the anteroom there arose a combination of scents, each crowding for prominence. Fish, seal, rabbits, an infinite array of old boots. I didn't linger there. The living room was quite respectable as igloos go. The floor was clean and so were the dishes. I immediately peeled off my parka and made myself at home. After a light lunch of boiled blackfish I gathered the children for a review of their Innuit prayers. In the evening the whole village crowded into the tiny igloo for singing, the rosary, and later, confessions, after the children had gone to bed.

Here I would like to introduce you to a peculiar law of contradiction in Eskimo family life. Spoiled babies up here do not grow into spoiled children. The Innuit family life has little in common with the white. In this the Eskimo is not necessarily to be pitied. The family code of the white is not, after all, the zenith of all family perfection. It is the result that counts. The Eskimo is not strictly logical, but he certainly gets results.

The adult Eskimos manifest little affection toward one another. Husband and wife in their mutual relations are very matter of fact. Men will come home after a week on their trap line and greet their anxious wives with nothing more than a nod and a smile. Rarely is there a courtship in our sense of the word before marriage. Even on the day of the wedding the couple will not walk home together.

Personally, I believe that the Eskimo is not fundamentally a stoic; rather he has taught himself to hide his affections on account of the complete lack of privacy in his way of life. His house is a one-room affair. Every act is exposed to the scrutiny of the numerous inmates. The result is a strict code of modesty and general good deportment. I have had dozens of opportunities to witness their home life every winter on the trail, and I have been continually edified by their good behavior.

If the grownups waste no affection among themselves, they certainly make up for it in the attention and solicitude they lavish on their children. The latest arrival is the uncrowned king of the household. The baby's slightest whim is gratified. At times these whims are expensive and destructive. I have known trappers noted for their common sense, coming home from a hard day's mushing and patiently lighting match after match simply because it tickles the fancy of the "small fry."

No matter what the little one wants it will be given him. The range of these wishes runs all the way from flashlights to scissors. The flashlight will eventually be broken to bits. The scissors will soon be laid aside, a little bloody, for discretion is taught speedily by experience. The baby finds out that scissors cut much as he finds out that stoves burn, or that puppy Malemutes bite. All are to be handled gingerly.

I marvel at the patience of Eskimo fathers buying dishes. An unbreakable dish would be a real triumph up here on the tundra. Traders tell me that many families lay in a whole new set of dishes every winter. I have often gone, however, to the homes of my people and found there the luxury of a single cup and perhaps a lone spoon. The father will tell me with a smile that he had more cups, but then the baby wanted them! Wooden bowls soon take the place of white man's dishes. They are frequently examples of exquisite handiwork, but not-so-exquisite cleanliness, so I usually pass them up, admiringly.

The baby can be most annoying to a new missionary in the field. He can reduce a serious catechetical session to a veritable witches' meeting merely by his vocalizing. I have tried many devious means to silence these little tyrants. The best I have found is to begin an Innuit hymn immediately when the tiny tenors warm up. Generally the mighty voice of a whole congregation will awe them somewhat. However, even this stratagem will sometimes fail, and an instruction which began on a suitably serious plane will end up in inglorious chaos. One can hardly order the culprit out of the house, for this would involve the departure of both father and mother to a lonely igloo. And the coming of a priest to a distant igloo village two or three times a year is an event which cannot be missed. Often it may be the only chance the Eskimo will have to make his yearly confession and Communion.

When all the pros and cons are carefully weighed the only solution appears to be "grin and bear it." The work here on the Yukon Delta seems to be primarily an apostolate for the babies, anyway. Most of these bland little agitators will never reach the use of reason. For countless hundreds the hands of the priest have opened the golden doors of the heavenly igloo, with no more cold, no more smells, no more hunger. I am not distressed, therefore, if the baby does have its way. I might add, too, that for all their spoiling in infancy, they become model children afterward — reverent and obedient to their parents, even to the extent of going to bed when they are told!

So bedtime came for all. I finally unrolled my sleeping bag and was soon asleep on a mattress in only relative ease, for two straight planks were under the mattress.

During the night I was awakened by a continuous smacking that seemed to come from pretty close to my head. I sat up and flashed my light around. There was nothing in sight, but the noise continued. It seemed to come from a harmless looking gunny sack. Curiosity finally conquered. I peered into the sack and found it full of blackfish. They were squirming around and smacking against one another in endless activity. These sturdy little creatures have been known to live for over a week out of water.

I went back to bed, and by a kind of a self-mesmerism reduced the smacking to a soothing lullaby and lulled by its exotic rhythm I slept until the first stirrings of the new day. I arose in the early light of morning, rolled up my sleeping bag and went out into the snow to wash up.

That may sound a little strange, but the water problem in Alaska is by no means the easiest to solve. It is not an extraordinary thing to wake up some cold Alaskan morning and find the water frozen in the washbasin — that is, if you are lucky enough to have water. But when one awakens in a small igloo with ten or twelve people rolling up their blankets and reindeer skins and only one washbasin of questionable antiseptic qualities, a brisk rubbing of the hands and face with pure fresh snow is a real tonic.

Water both for drinking and for washing, however, is of prime necessity even in a cold climate. The Eskimos go to a lot of trouble to fill their water barrel either with river water or with lake ice. Snow water might for all practical purposes have been distilled; it does not satisfy the thirst. On the Yukon all one needs to do is cut a hole in the ice, dip, and come up with a brimming bucket. Coastal towns such as Kotzebue have certain fresh-water lakes several miles distant from the village. Here the ice is sawed in fifty or hundred-pound blocks and hauled in by dog team. It costs about $4.50 a ton, C.O.D. Ice cut in early winter is the best and cleanest. Later on, with deep snow and successive thaws, it can develop a distinctive if not unpleasant taste.

It is really astonishing how much water Eskimo children and men on the trail drink. Naturally, a child romping about in the snow in a heavy parka perspires freely and needs to be refilled.

And pushing a sled, or plowing through soft snow on snowshoes to set his traps is hard on the man's water supply. What is more, an Eskimo will not hesitate to satisfy his thirst. I have seen him leisurely stop his team in the coldest kind of weather, unleash his sled cover — always a cold undertaking in subzero weather — and with all the time in the world, patiently rummage out a tiny ax and just as patiently cut a hole through the ice. All for an ice-cold drink on the trail. The same thing is done for tea water at lunchtime. Many of the Eskimos now have thermos bottles. They will use them for a time, but gradually the old method of teapot and melted ice is returning. "Anyway," he shrugs, "at midday the dogs must be rested."

The whites sometimes condemn the native because his garments lack that smooth finish of a dry-cleaning establishment. Let them live as the Eskimos do out in a winter igloo with every ounce of water melted by a tiny stove from ice blocks! What is more, let a white go out on a trapping line with a group of Eskimos for a week or so. He will return the most unkempt of the group.

After my brisk and incomplete morning toilet, I strolled a bit in the crisp freshness of the morning. It was not hard to pray here, to prepare for the great moment of the Mass to come. After a few deep breaths and a few deeper prayers, I returned and ducked my way into the crowded igloo.

It was packed for Mass. Poor ventilation and the excessive heat which naturally rose to the small arched region of the ceiling made me dizzy. But it didn't bother my servers. One was a lad from the same igloo, the other from a neighboring one. Both were alert. Black eyes snapped with intense interest and pride in their job. It is heart-warming to see how these lads learn and retain the intricacies of the Latin responsories, and to see the quick joy they take in serving the *agayulerta's* Mass.

When one first comes in contact with the smooth, expression-less face of an Eskimo boy one is inclined to think the lad lacks the glee and easy unconcern which distinguishes youth from maturity. However, a missionary has a chance to break down the barrier which blocks the approach of a white into the warmth of an Eskimo family circle. The priest is able to see the Eskimo boy as he really is — happy and carefree.

One of the greatest blessings of our work up here in the Arctic is the fact that we are trusted. This is evidenced in a thousand ways. A good example of this is the radiant simplicity and lack of restraint which the children show in the presence of a priest. The roistering welcome they give me as my team ribbons over a neighboring hill of snow always gives me the first warmth against the chill of the trail. I can turn over my tired Malemutes to the boys and know that they will be efficiently unharnessed, tied, and fed while I retire at once to the shelter of their family home.

I have had the opportunity to study these lads in those fields of activity which a boy loves best. I have been his companion both in winter and summer. During the past several years we have hunted and fished together, skated and snowshoed together, mushed and bivouacked together. Needless to say I have not had the slightest trouble finding the wholesomeness and cheerful disposition which is the natural right of every boy.

But how does the youth of the Arctic differ from his American brother? Of course, living as he does so close to nature, restraint of any kind is irksome. He loves the open, loves movement and play. A twenty-mile jaunt for game will not tire him half as much as an hour's work on a woodpile. However, he prefers work of any kind to school. In the classroom, drawing and music are his forte, arithmetic his weakness.

Lacking the many sources of artificial amusements so prevalent in more modern cultures, he is forced to fall back on his own ingenuity to supply his recreation. Acting comes as natural to him as water to a duck. Endless practice and a natural creative instinct have made him a deadly mimic. His acute powers of observation never miss an oddity in another's make-up. Mannerisms, especially of the whites, are reproduced with exquisite artistry. It is somewhat surprising to see even the soberest old chief double up with merriment at these exhibitions. Naturally they are at their best in imitating bird calls. Many a royal meal has flown out of the northern sky in response to some irresistible call from the ground.

The trait that has impressed me most in these children of the tundra is their resourcefulness. In this I think they have the edge over the boys of the States. There is no gainsaying the blunt fact that Alaska is a country of emergency and disappointment. But there are few sudden situations that can ruffle the placid serenity of an Eskimo. And as a consequence, from every emergency he comes out somehow or another the victor. There have been a few occasions on the trail when I would have panicked, but for the calm reassurance of my boy guide. What I had considered a real adventure was to him a mere incident of the trail. This imperturbability flows through the whole of his life. He loves nature, takes from her what he thinks he needs, and leaves the rest to the God who cares for salmon, the fox, the goose, and for himself.

After Mass I repacked my kit and laid it beside my bedroll. I noticed that it was quickly picked up and carried out through the entrance. This told me that my sled and dogs were being readied for the trail.

But a man on the morning trail is only as good as his breakfast, so I proceeded to make myself a good musher, at least for that morning. Breakfast in a crowded igloo is an experience all by itself, but more of that later. I hurried through, paid my *devoirs* to the father and mother and kids, promised to return as soon as possible, and waved myself away along the wet and difficult trail toward my next village.

8. Kotzebue

I HAVE often noted before that Alaska has a way of teaching one to trust implicitly in divine providence. There is so much up here that one cannot control, that sooner or later one comes to depend largely, if not completely, on God's dispositions of things. I found occasion to make use of that lesson when I got word of my transfer from Akulurak to Kotzebue.

It is true that I had had two operations in rather quick succession, but it was equally true that I had recovered completely from them. Or so I thought. But my superiors didn't think quite the same as I, for they believed that I should be relieved from any more heavy trail work. In spite of the fact that I liked that kind of work, and liked the stark simplicity and quick response of the lonely Eskimo villages, I almost automatically fell back on the lesson that Alaska has taught me, and made my preparations for the change. It was hard, however, to turn over my dog teams to my successor.

And then, too, Kotzebue is not exactly a heaven on earth. It is far north; north of the Arctic Circle, in fact. Besides that, it is in the heart of Quaker country — having relatively few Catholics. That would mean a continual strain in order to maintain such things as Church ceremonials and feast-day celebrations which had become so much of my life at Akulurak.

Anyway, the lesson held good, and here I was at Kotzebue, with every day showing me more and more of God's wisdom and His ways.

He gives one such swift and suddenly beautiful rewards. As you know, the arctic priest has his share of "ups and downs."

His Eskimo youngsters, sometimes so phenomenally dull and other times so surprisingly wise and sophisticated, can get on his nerves. The older people with their strange combination of the serpent and the dove can make him pause sickly in the midst of his work. But there is always something that sweeps like a cool summer breeze over the fever of his toil — and it is usually the wind of the Holy Spirit.

This often happens during a lone midweek Mass with only the whisper of falling snow to furnish the background. Or it might come when God's quick grace opens a troubled soul to healing words. And it always happens at the baptism of a tiny baby who almost immediately afterward rises from the dirt and suffering of its earthly life to the pure light of heaven.

It happened just the other day. A little orphan girl, unwanted by her mother, unclaimed by her father, through some strange disposition of God's providence found her way into the Mission. I baptized her, and within a half hour, she was free of this strange land that could not sustain her life.

I had feared that my days at Kotzebue would bring with them too much inactivity, but, as is usual with such fears, it was unfounded. Activity comes in the most unsuspected ways. I was not here long, for instance, before I began to see that the town's ax of justice fell with astonishing dispatch. An Eskimo had been sentenced by the judge to three months in jail, simply for setting a trap at the wrong time. His sentence rested on very shaky circumstantial evidence, which came to light only after the accomplished fact. Then a week or so later another Eskimo was sentenced to a year in jail for assault. He unexpectedly demanded a trial by jury. I haven't the faintest idea where this simple man got such a complicated idea, but he got it. I was appointed his defense attorney.

The work of choosing a jury went on with all the legal formality of a white man's court. The lines were strongly drawn in the whole affair, because it was basically Eskimo versus white. One of the local storekeepers was the plaintiff. It is superfluous to add that my cheering section was made up almost exclusively of the native population.

The day of the trial came swiftly. The marshal's office had not bulged like that in years. The improvised courtroom was hardly big enough for the jurors, let alone the spectators who squeezed into it. I picked an advantageous place from which I could keep my eyes on both the jury and the witnesses. The court was just about to be called when we discovered that one of the Eskimo women jurors was missing. It was decided immediately to arrest her for contempt of court, and substitute another juror in her place. The marshal puffed around one corner of the building in search of his prospective prisoner, and she puffed around another. The judge then departed on his bicycle to intercept the marshal. Finally after fifteen minutes more delay the trial proceeded.

The jurors were sworn in, the witnesses called one after another. These I cross-examined carefully — two native boys so scared at all the formality that they could hardly talk. Then I called the defendant to the stand, and told him to relate his story truthfully. This he did, so simply and eloquently that he actually needed no other defense. It was plain that the man was innocent. I summed up the case afterward and pointed out that very much was being made of very little. The plaintiff replied, but without much effect. The jury brought in its vote acquittal in not more than half an hour.

As I expected, the white population discussed the case with a certain amount of heat. Within three days, however, it was a forgotten thing, and my Eskimo friend could go about his affairs as a free man.

The trial hardly ended when the blizzards set in. Huge snow-drifts that a week of east wind had laboriously piled up were demolished in an hour, and new ones substituted for them. The scourging north wind attacked the hard undersnow and sent tiny pellets bulleting through the air with a refinement of torture that is hard to believe, much less describe.

I took advantage of the foul weather to do my immediate visiting. This kind of a wind keeps people home where I could find them. So I set off with my Mass pictures and a stereoscope. At my first stop a little group of Eskimos gathered about me. They looked with impressed awe on the pictures of solemn Mass being celebrated in beautiful churches. I explained the Mass as picture followed picture, and saw that it was worth much more than a short, freezing trip just to watch the expressions of joy and wonder on the faces around me. One young wife found the usual Eskimo grunt too inadequate for her sentiments; she turned to me and said, with wide eyes, "My, it must be fun being a priest." I looked at her and smiled. "More than you know," I said, and started home alone. Her words lived in my mind for a long time. It is fun to be a priest, but beginnings are not always such. I remember my first Alaskan parish. It was at Pilot Station on the Yukon.

I had slipped on some ice and wrenched my knee. I was alone with the blizzard and too little wood. I hobbled over to my bunk and put a tight bandage around the sprain. It had brought on a nervous attack of shivering that didn't help my hard-won patience much. I labored my bed over near the food and fuel, and lay quietly until I saw my last stick of wood go up in smoke. When I felt the cold creeping toward me I got up (not without appropriate grunts) and struggled over to the bell. Seldom has there been such deadly earnest in the ringing of a bell. In a few minutes my room was packed with excited natives; "*Agayulerta,*

he sick — *choknok!*" From then on there was no worry about
either food or fuel.

After two weeks, during which the weather had cleared somewhat, I could hobble around with an improvised cane. Then one
day the north wind returned, bringing with it a grim gift of
30-below-zero weather. I was stoking my stove like a locomotive
fireman and thinking, "what a jolly time to get a sick call!" when
a knock came.

It was Peter Tutluk, swathed in furs frozen from his forty-mile
trek from Takchak, northeast of Pilot Station.

"Nick Coffee, he sick. Sometime he die," he said through his
furs.

"What's the trouble," I asked.

"Heart; he beat only sometimes."

I looked out my window onto the trail. Driving snow was
hurtling down from the north in blinding drifts. I would have to
face that for forty miles if I went to the sick man.

"How many dogs have you, Pete?"

"Good dogs; maybe nine. Me take you?"

"You will take *us*, Peter," I answered.

"I take good care of you and Jesus."

He turned and went out, and I made my preparations. In
twenty minutes we were on the trail.

It is needless to describe the trip. Due to my knee injury I
had to ride. Because of the past two-week stretch of inactivity
and inside warmth, I felt the cold as I have never felt it before
or since. The wind simply disregarded my furs. I could feel its
fingers on the very nerve centers of my bones. At times I thought
my eyes would freeze to my head. Each hour felt like a day,
and for eight terrible hours we faced that north wind. As I look
back on it I have to laugh at how certain I was that any minute
I would cease being a man and turn into a cake of ice. On and

on we went. As dark approached the dogs picked up speed and the wind got colder, if that was possible.

But if that trip was cold, the warmth of my reception at the village was enough to thaw me out. The whole village was gathered to welcome me. It was gratifying to receive such signs of respect and admiration from the usually imperturbable native. I went straight to the sick man, and after some questioning I found out that, though he had been receiving the sacraments for the past five years, he had never been baptized! I instructed him briefly and baptized him. During his reception of the rest of the last rites his joy and peace made an impression that will stay with me as long as I live. Yes, it is fun to be a priest.

9. Play Master

I HAVE had occasion several times before to remark on the swift joy and absolute abandon with which the Eskimo can and does enter into his playtime. Such times are almost always unpredictable, ushered in as they so frequently are by sudden temperature changes, or unlooked-for good luck on the hunt. This impromptu celebration, of course, does not include the more elaborate "snow fiestas" they put on to commemorate more important occasions, such as large feast days of the Church.

It does not take a new Alaskan missionary long to see and respect one of the Eskimo's prominent celebration talents, music. I have noticed that the successful missionary invariably capitalizes on this excellent trait in the Eskimo character. The old Italian and French missionaries were themselves good musicians and employed their art incessantly to win over the people of the North.

They translated the best hymns of the Christian Brothers' Hymnal into decasyllabic Eskimo and the melody seems to be improved by the version. Father Lonneux has gone so far as to duplicate an entire Eskimo hymnal with most remarkable results. His work has become the standard text for almost 3000 Eskimos on the Lower Yukon. One has only to listen to the *Adeste Fideles*," or "Mother Dear, O Pray for Me," as sung in Chiniliak, Akulurak, Mountain Village, Hooper Bay, or Nelson Island, to realize what success can be achieved by community singing in Eskimo land.

In the beautiful Church of St. Mary at Akulurak between

three and four hundred Eskimos gather for the feasts of Christmas and Easter. When these deep-chested children of the North raise their completely un-self-conscious voices in the ringing melodies of "Silent Night," and *"Adeste Fideles,"* the celebrant at Mass is thrilled through and through. All the voices seem to funnel directly to the altar, and the officiating priest gets the full benefit of the echoing emotions of his flock. What is said of Akulurak can just as well be said of the other places. On big feast days the Eskimos, one and all, sing, and sing from the heart. Singing is one of the most important functions of their religion, as indeed it should be.

Up here, above the Arctic Circle, the natives are the same as on the Yukon. The Quakers early saw the importance of singing and it is the one attraction in their otherwise rather drab services. Their well-drilled part chorus is something to be envied. When Father Frank Menager came to Kotzebue he at once set to work showing these people how to sing high Mass. They took to it as naturally as a duck to water. The Latin words were no impediment. In no time high Mass was a regular Sunday service. Many families had their own organs and spent hours mastering the more difficult parts.

If sacred music reveals the really deep emotional nature of the Eskimo, it is profane music that shows his lighter side. I reconditioned an old organ and reserved it for popular songs after our evening services. The good wholesome fun that comes from "Songs the Whole World Sings" is as real here as it used to be around the American family circle years before the appearance of the radio.

I have noticed in the past that a people of leisure instinctively turns to music. The Eskimo is no exception. Some years ago I had an old banjo gathering dust in the house. One of the boys begged me to let him borrow it. I asked him if he knew how to play. No, but he would learn. He took the instrument out with him on a hunting trip. Three months later he came back with the banjo mastered. He could pick up a melody from a phonograph and render it in faultless style.

At Holy Cross and Akulurak the mission boys are constantly strumming a banjo, ukulele, or guitar. With no help from anyone, they will sit for hours fingering the strings until they get the notes for which they are listening. Little by little they patiently construct a melody and before you know it, their fingers are traveling deftly over the strings, bringing out all kinds of harmony. Long, blizzardy nights lose their dreariness when musical instruments are handy.

The Eskimo musical ability is put to good use in the main celebration of the North, the Potlatch, or *Ka-ze-ok*. I call to mind an Akulurak celebration a few years ago. The year had been hard, with much sickness, little success at the traps, and a scarcity of food. But, with the strange wisdom of these northern people, one of the Akulurak villagers insisted on celebrating the prowess of young son as a hunter; a potlatch there must be, and no excuse would suffice. A potlatch is usually the celebration of plenty. But it was by no means out of place in that period of relative hunger, for it is not only a time of giving, but of receiving. And, too, the morale of the people needed a lift. So a potlatch was planned.

Perhaps it is wise to give a correct view of this celebration. In the old days before the traders had settled in Alaska a potlatch was a time when two different tribes or villages came together in the style of the old-time country fair. Bartering as such, however, was strictly forbidden. The whole atmosphere was that of a feast day — a day of giving and receiving presents. There was no medium of exchange. The coastal Eskimo brought along their catch of seal, *laftak, mukluk,* and pokes of seal and whale oil. The natives of the interior reciprocated with moose, bear, beaver, wolf, and wolverine skins. It was a very happy and useful exchange. All these articles are essential for both peoples in this cold country. Whites sometimes are inclined to think that a potlatch simply means a promiscuous giving and feasting with consequent impoverishment. This may sometimes happen but it is a degeneration from the old-time potlatch and shows a lack of proper management on the part of the respective chiefs.

The details of the potlatch are interesting. There is a time-honored ritual that must be adhered to. First of all, messengers must be sent to the village in question to invite them to the feast. At this time, too, a smooth and tactful intimation of the kinds of presents that would be acceptable is given. The interchange of presents is always made in the name of the children or of the community. The little daughter or son of a certain potlatch donor would be very happy to receive fawn skins for his parka, wolverine for the hood, and so on. The *Kazim* is badly in need of a bearskin for the entrance; or the old light is simply no good any more, and a gas lamp would be so very welcome.

After the messengers have made the announcement of the coming potlatch the interminable rehearsals of song and dance take place. Almost every night at sundown the people repair to the *Kazim* to repeat the various songs until every note harmonizes with the beat of the drum and the movement of the dance. During the rehearsal old men sit by carving out fantastic masks. The chief of the village and the master of the feast sit at the ends of a semicircle. The singers are ranged in between. The women and children are scattered around more or less haphazardly on the raised tier around the sides of the *Kazim*. The dance itself always takes place at full moon. As the time draws near the excitement increases. Women hurry to finish little presents of needlework. The men give double duty to their nets so that plenty of fish will be on hand. Young men gather all the wood they can get their hands on. The guests must be treated with becoming hospitality to avoid the dreaded stigma of stinginess.

Finally the eve of this particular potlatch arrived. Fresh messengers were sent to tell the people of Alaranak that all was in readiness. From Alaranak seventeen teams departed in solemn procession. Halfway to their destination they were met by more messengers, and small presents like tobacco were interchanged. As the visitors came within sight of Akulurak, still more messengers ran out to welcome them. These foot messengers were to say that Akulurak had no bread or fish (meaning that they had plenty) but come anyway — you are most welcome to our humble village. Finally all the visiting teams raced into the village and were met at the nearest house by all the men, and led at once into the different houses for a sip of tea.

Then began a time of feasting, small gossip, and good cheer that lasted until sundown. The home villagers then betook themselves to the *Kazim*. The visitors afterward entered the *Kazim* singly or in twos, bearing presents which were deposited in the center of the room. Each present was the signal for a resounding song of gratitude. When all the presents had been piled high in the middle and all were comfortably seated, songs and dances began in earnest and lasted until midnight. The next evening the procedure was reversed with the visitors on the receiving end.

The songs are introduced by an expert singer who begins his intonation in a sort of a monotone, giving the general theme. At a signal from the feathered baton of the dance master, the dancer takes her place and then with the crash of three big drums the singers begin. The tempo increases as the song moves along.

The dancer sways her body gracefully, portraying as vividly as possible some incident of native life. The singers themselves sway back and forth to the time of the drums, giving an illusion of action over the whole interior of the *Kazim*. From the smallest to the oldest, there is enthusiastic participation in the dance. It is no mere spectacle.

And thus the potlatch is carried on, amid celebration and singing and general good will. It is a gracious and friendly way to combine the trading so necessary among the natives up here with genuine good fun and relaxation.

But even such an elaborate celebration was not enough to satisfy the Eskimo hunger for fun. Before long they began to talk among themselves about another "fiesta." They finally spoke to me about it, and I suggested, since they already had a pot-latch, and since it was a lean year for presents, that they hold one of their traditional mask dances. And furthermore, since Lent up here is observed with apostolic vigor, why not introduce it with the traditional Mardi Gras? They fell in with the idea immediately, and preparations were just as immediately under-taken for their dance.

A mask dance on the Yukon is intimately allied with native customs and traditions. Formerly the dance was nothing else but the expression of a potent medicine man's dreams. The strength of the medicine man was judged from the ability of his dance to foretell favorable trapping conditions, and perhaps, even bring them about. If, for example, his dance portrayed the antics of a fox, and afterward fox were plentiful, the medicine of this man was reputed very powerful indeed, and his services were carefully sought out. Lately the medicine man is dying out of Eskimo life, but the songs and dances remain.

Once a mask dance is decided upon, it takes about two or three weeks to round it into shape. Of course, just as in amateur performances outside, the rehearsals are brimming with fun and roughhouse gaiety. The songs, endlessly repetitious as they are, are not very difficult to learn. The dance itself is more so. The dancer's movements must be done in perfect time with the drums and song and still include a very humorous and extremely realistic pantomime representing the animal in question. It begins with a slow, solemn beat of the drums. Gradually the tempo is increased until it becomes almost frenzied. The length of the dance depends on the crowd. They will sometimes keep the dancer going until he drops from sheer exhaustion. The cries of the dancer are wonderfully true to life. The duck, the goose, or the swan actually seem present, and almost make you reach instinctively for your gun.

Of course, just as in the Mardi Gras, one of the principal elements of the dance is the mask itself. The natives generally make these out of the stump of a birch tree. This wood is used because it is round and will not crack. The carving of the mask is done in the *Kazim* at rehearsals. Heads of bear, beaver, crow, seal, fox, or any other familiar animal are ingeniously carved and painted with a mixture taken from crushed rock.

Dances are portioned out to practically every one of dancing ability in the village. The men choose their lady partners. Generally one couple, and at most two, hold the floor at one time. The man with mask kneels in the center of the *Kazim*. The woman stands a few feet behind. Both carry in each hand fans made out of goose or swan feathers. The woman is never masked. Rather, she is decked out in her best furs. Her head is adorned with a wolf band studded with feathers, something on the order of the Indian headdress. It is the business of the woman to copy the movements of the masked man in front of her. She imitates the comic gestures of her masked partner with a gracefulness and artistry that is marvelous to an outsider.

The *Kazim* itself is decorated with the express purpose of giving the impression that one is out in the open air with the sky overhead. Long light laths, such as are used in making fish traps, are run from the sides to the center of the ceiling. A cord is tied to the sticks in the center, and this is so manipulated that the entire improvised ceiling can rise and fall to the measure of the dance. The sticks are studded with tiny feathers to represent stars. Bad omen is portended if one of these little feathery stars falls on a person during the dance. An eerie effect is produced by this combined movement of the dancer, the chorus, and the ceiling. It is impossible not to be carried away by the spirit of the song.

When all the preparations are made, the whole village resorts to the *Kazim* at sundown. Unlike the potlatch dancers, the men now range themselves on the first tier which encircles the entire *Kazim*. The women and children sit directly underneath them. The floor is left free for the dancers. Just over the door a long pole runs the entire width of the room. On this are fixed thirty or forty candles. When all are seated, the candles are ceremoniously lighted in hushed expectation.

Suddenly from the vestibule of the *Kazim* the hoarse growl of a bear is heard. The unmistakable pawing and scratching of a bear searching for food is then heard about the entrance. Then amidst the cries of all, a bear-masked native comes hurtling through the entrance. Several young men jump up to attack him. With everybody shouting, babies crying, and general clamor, a bear assault is staged. The bear is finally wounded or killed, quiet is restored, and a lady dancer takes her place. The chief motions to the drummers and the dance is on.

Sometimes the masked native will come flying out of the corner of the *Kazim*. Then his cries will be a perfect mimicry of a wounded goose in flight.

What impressed me most in this dance was how perfectly every man, woman, and child enters into the spirit of the occasion. Unlike the popular white dance, which is nothing but a stereotyped, sentimental affair, the native dances are what one could well term a native light opera. Clever acting and pantomime, choral singing of astonishing perfection. The whole thing cannot help but inspire the spectator with sheer awe at its significance and artistry.

This was a good introduction to the rigors of Lent. But it by no means exhausts the Eskimo's ability to play. The following Christmas was celebrated by a full week of games whose rivalry and excitement outdid anything I ever saw in the States. After the religious exercises of Christmas Day, the proclamation was read; a full week of contests and games was to follow. Trapping and fishing, all work of any kind was unhesitatingly pushed aside.

The few light hours of the days that followed were occupied by races of various kinds, in good weather and bad. The big event, of course, was the dog derby, consisting of the fastest teams of the best mushers. But this by no means comprised all the dog racing. Everybody, young and old, men and women, entered some kind of race, whether it was the three dog race, the five, or more. There were at least five different sets of entries for each event. In a full week there is plenty of time for everything, even for a steaming cup of coffee between the matches.

Whenever the huge American flag was planted on the beach, activities resumed. There were snowshoe contests, ski runs, foot and three-legged races. One of the special features was the camping trip match. Sleds were loaded with all the necessary equipment for the trail. A five-mile course was laid out, ending at the starting point. The winner had to make the course, return, set up his tent with lightning speed, and get his fire going. This is no small feat, incidentally, when there is a twenty-five mile an hour wind blowing down the arctic coast.

When darkness stopped the outdoor games, the whole village gathered in the school. Games and feats of strength went on till midnight. White spectators are invariably amazed at the variety of sports as well as at the display of muscle and sheer dexterity of these stocky and clumsy looking people of mine. And here again everybody is given a chance. There is a complete lack of hurry or any sign of impatience to get things done. The almost automaton efficiency of similar events of the States never appears. If one event is not finished one day it is imperturbably scheduled for completion on the next.

At midnight the prizes were awarded. Blue and red ribbons were pinned on grinning Eskimo laddies by solemn Eskimo lassies. The procedure was reversed, of course, when the girls won their prizes.

On the last night of festivities things were particularly animated. After a couple of hours in a room filled with two hundred fur-clad Eskimos I began to yearn for the starry freshness of the night. I returned to my room, warm with joy at the thought of my people's happiness. I flipped the radio to see how the rest of the world was enjoying Christmas spirit. Rackety jazz! I twirled the dial — fifteen ships sunk, 345 planes downed! I sighed and turned the radio off. And I thought of the old man who told me the day before: "White, he funny. Me, me no think too much; me do, but me happy!" I sighed to myself as I turned in that night — "How true, how very true."

10. Frozen Foods, Ltd.

SELDOM has Kotzebue seen such a glorious fall as the one we just had. The sound and lagoon froze into one shimmering sheet of glass. Cold, clear days with little snow made ideal conditions for herding the reindeer close to the village. The first of November came, and with it came the "Reindeer Chief," swinging into the village with his long string of dogs. Deer were at hand for the slaughter, and all the villagers were hustling to go out. Every available team was readied, and trails appeared like magic where no trails had been before.

The government is doing its utmost to preserve the reindeer in Alaska; and with reason. They furnish plenty and comfort for the Eskimo. Fawn skins mean parkas for every member of the family. And without these the native, especially the native children, easily become chilled and rapidly develop tuberculosis.

Older skins make excellent mattresses. They are also bleached and used for the uppers of summer and fall *mukluks*. An Eskimo home has plenty of uses for raw leather. The reindeer legs are perfect for the legs of winter boots; sinew gives strong and durable thread; the tallow furnishes lard and soap; and last but certainly not least, the meat is a very welcome reprieve from the somewhat prosaic diet of sea foods.

So, when the hunt bustle reached its height, the arctic pastor joined in. He, too, needed meat for the winter. A daily fare of fish soon borders on monotony, shall we say. Fish for dinner, fish for supper; fried, then boiled, and then aromatically fried again; it may be good for the brains, but it becomes decidedly bad for the palate. After a few months of such uninspired and

84

uninspiring diet, even the pastor finds the reindeer hunt a thing of vast importance.

Off I went, therefore, to join my departing flock. It was a brisk, cold day, and furs were in order. I was prospecting for a ride when one of my parishioners came whirling down a hill riding an empty sled behind eleven well-matched Malemutes. I piled in.

At this early season the dogs are usually soft, and quickly slow down. Luckily our team had been a bit hardened by frequent trips to the ice lake. So we gaily whipped along, passing every team in sight. A three hours' run brought us to the reindeer camp. Eskimo hospitality had gone before us. Our arrival there was greeted with smiles and calls, and delicious reindeer stew with steaming cups of coffee. It takes a musher, fresh from a cold trail and chilled to the bone to appreciate such culinary triumphs.

Later the deer were slaughtered, skinned, and hung up to freeze. The reindeer boys thoroughly knew their business and did their work in subzero weather without a thought for the cold. The deer at this time of year are fat and in the best condition for killing. As winter progresses they thin down to sheer muscle and bone, for the very effort needed to exist is hard; sometimes the deer have to paw through a foot or more of snow just to eat.

Finally the hunt was over. Returning against the wind with the sun already hiding behind the horizon was no pleasant jaunt. The wind off Kotzebue Sound, sharpened up by its long sweep across the Arctic Ocean from Siberia, has a toothiness that penetrates even the fur parka. But we finally arrived, and proceeded to replenish the village larder with some much-needed meat. All of which called for a celebration that night. But more about that later.

The work is done: everybody is tired. But my people have their deep, quiet smile of gratitude to God and their own strange country for this bounty that would do so much to make the long harsh winter and freakish spring more bearable. For any help over those months is of greater importance in proportion as the time is hard. But with this plenty, and with the vision of summer in the offing, even the short days and long, cold nights seem to lose much of their dulling impact. It is summer that keeps the land and people alive — offering with lavish hand almost endless opportunity for berries, greens, fish, whales, and later, birds.

So finally, summer comes again, and with it fishing and whaling. Ice chunks have been swept away. Only a few vanishing snowbanks are left near the shore. These afford fresh water to those who live so close to the sea. Tents of the fishers are erected on both sides of the Kotzebue spit, and nets are daily loaded with deep red salmon. There is no work schedule and no darkness. During this time of the year the sun shines twenty-four hours a day, so the Eskimos eat when they are hungry and sleep when they are tired. Few go to bed before midnight and few awake before the morning is well along.

During this season the Eskimo children have the time of their lives. Their diet is rich; no school to plague them, no wood to cut, no regular hours. They wander happy and carefree around the village. Planes are met, visitors scrutinized, boats are watched, duck and goose eggs gathered on the tundra, fresh fish bolted without limit. The capacity of these little Eskimo tummies is amazing. They seem to have the receptivity of a smokehouse.

Kotzebue, incidentally, is the only arctic village in Alaska that has the distinction of having a catechism class. I might add that the boys and girls are proud of their unique position. In early

Ursuline Nuns — Akulurak

Brother Murphy at the Fish Wheel

Easter Parade

Alaskan Territorial Guard

winter as an inducement to diligent study and frequent attendance, the pastor held out the promise of magnificent presents
to be distributed on Christmas Day. About the only thing
actually magnificent about the presents was the way they were
received. The sun is not the only source of warmth in this cold
and beautiful land.

But after Christmas the problem was how to keep their
interest from flagging. I took a leaf from the book of St. Paul,
and became all things to all children. That is to say, I painted
for their vivid imaginations the glorious picture of a gigantic
picnic to be held in early summer, as soon as the berries and
wild rhubarb were ripe. Only the most diligent and industrious,
of course, could even be considered for this wonderful outing.
When the time finally arrived, I solemnly pronounced, before
those strained oval faces, that everybody had been diligent, and
that everybody would go picnicking the next morning.

July 8 shone clear. Our boat had been caulked and painted.
The engine was overhauled. So we gathered around — fifteen
strong excluding the pilot and engineer. Our objective was that
wonderful place — "Anywhere." It had to have a fine, clean beach
and be out of sight of the village.

Our picnic supplies were few — some cups, a little sugar, a
half pound of cocoa, two loaves of bread, a can of jam, and a jar
of peanut butter. If you don't think that was riches beyond our
fondest dreams, you should have seen the wondering joy on the
faces of the children when I ostentatiously flourished these supplies on board.

We loaded the boat before the wondering and envious eyes
of the rest of the villagers. This is fundamentally a Quaker
settlement, by the way, and the frivolous and luxurious habits
of the Catholic pastor are openly frowned upon — and secretly
envied. The boat moved off; the motor hummed, and with a

shout to the Quaker lads and lassies solemnly lining the bank
we departed for that magic place out of sight of here. Up before
the broad sweep of Kotzebue houses we passed. Our little boat
was heavily loaded so I hugged the shoreline as a safety
measure.

Kotzebue lingered long in the distance behind us. For a time
it seemed to squat placidly on the water itself, and finally faded
from view. The youngsters were in glorious spirits and chided
me for a poor shot as I missed two blasts at some fast-moving
pintails. I silenced them immediately, though, with a lucky shot
into a flock of sea gulls. I remarked with solemn unconcern, and
considerable prevarication, that I had even picked my bird out
of a group of twenty-five!

But, heave ho there! In the excitement of watching flying
ducks, we had swerved dangerously near a long salmon net
and just missed snarling it with our propeller.

It is amusing to compare the remarks of Eskimo children with
those of white children on a similar outing. Conversation here
ranged almost exclusively within the boundaries of hunting and
fishing, from muskrat to the whale. It is from offhand remarks
of these children that I often pick up details of a chase that
I would probably never learn from their elders.

We landed near a beautiful mountain stream with a perfect
beach. The kids scrambled off immediately on a tour of investi-
gation, but soon returned with the atmosphere behind them
black with mosquitoes. I hastily made a smudge while they
scurried to prepare for swimming and wading. Arctic waters
are distinctively chilly, but Eskimo blood is thick and warm.
Yet even this thick warm blood was not sufficient to keep them
in the water very long, and back they came, clamoring for
cocoa, bread, and jam.

After a quick and efficient lunch, I suggested that a trip

further up the coast might be nice — and had to protect myself
in the ensuing rush to the boat. The sea had become a huge
mass of undulating liquid glass. So out we headed into the sea
and the wind, to shake the carnivorous hoards of mosquitoes
that had settled on us. The wind of the sea did what smudges
and slappings had not done, and in no time at all we were free
of these pernicious pests.

Now that we had rid ourselves of them, I settled back to
enjoy what I can very well believe to be the most beautiful
scene in the Arctic — a deep-green ocean shimmering under the
golden light of a setting sun which never allows the day to die
completely, but lengthens its beautiful, breathless evening into
the fiery glory of another morning. The shoreline was bounded
by one low line of foothills; beyond them the Kobuk Range rose
to rugged and beautiful heights. As I looked off into the chang-
ing purple of these mountains I wondered which was the mountain of jade so often spoken of by the Kobuk miners.

After a couple of hours of exquisite boating we landed against
a tall jutting cliff where wild rhubarb is plentiful. The youngsters
dashed off in all directions, soon returning with fat stalks of
sweet rhubarb and other greens whose names I cannot possibly
guess at in English. The Eskimos pack them in seal oil and hold
them against the attacks of their constant enemy, winter.

This is what you might call the picnic for fun. There is another
kind of picnic in which the Eskimo, with his genius for play,
brings work and fun together in a truly masterful fashion. It
is usually a family affair, coming soon after the summer fishing
is over, when the berries become plentiful beyond wildest
imaginings. Things are piled high and wide in a homemade
rowboat — tent, a little dry fish and seal oil, buckets for berries,
and children in every empty nook and cranny. Around the event
hovers a wonderful aura of leisure. Mama has no club meetings

to attend; papa is his own boss and free to do what he wants; and the kids, well, their only hurry is to get started.

So, down the river they go, completely oblivious to the sheets of rain that might fall for as much as five days during this time of the year. They just pull their whale-gut parkas a little tighter and grin something about the rain being wet. Birds of all descriptions are flying around; sea gulls, marsh hawks, ducks with their little ones, several varieties of snipe, loons, owls, and a host of small darting birds that I will not presume to name because of their number.

Finally, after a number of hours, six or eight — it doesn't matter as the time seldom enters into the Eskimo computation — high ground is reached; a likely place for berries. As they draw into the bank, a flock of long-legged cranes slowly take wing and lumber off. They have been feasting on berries, and now rather grumpily yield the field to the visitors.

The children scatter, chasing little ducks, eating berries, completely at home in the tundra. A tent is pitched, water carried, wood chopped, and then begins the carefree job of picking berries.

Salmon berries are red and almost as big as a strawberry. Blueberries are about the size of a gooseberry and have the tart taste of a wild grape. Blackberries look much like the blue, but are hard and almost tasteless. Cranberries are like our own cranberries in the States. It often happens that the pickers will not have to move out of one berry field to get all these different kinds of berries at once.

Time flows gently over the pickers. Hunting ducks will be a pleasant diversion. Then, too, a net can be set in the river with full assurance of catching some kind of fish, generally, at this time of the year, pink or silver salmon. The silent tundra has enveloped this family. It is a marvel to see how easily both the children and the grownups are amused. The toys for the youngsters will be a baby gull or duckling. Mice will be shot with bow and arrow. There are no worries, either financial or otherwise. Prayer comes simply and naturally. Often the clear young voices of the children can be heard rendering a lovely hymn through the silence. God is somehow very close to these people, especially at these times when they are making such a work of art out of the work of their hands.

After a hearty meal in the evening, the music maker brings out his accordian. A circle of brown smiling faces forms in the firelight, and the dance begins. Then half a dozen of the menfolk might engage in a blanket tossing to the huge amusement of the whole group. The picnic goes on, maybe for one night, maybe for a week. No one cares, as long as the berries are picked and stored, as long as the fun lasts.

And so the Eskimo eats. Reindeer meat, all kinds of fish, birds, berries, greens, eggs. All from that strange, unpromising land which really fulfills so many promises. They gather their food with a smile, eat it with a smile, and are thankful with a smile. It is all part of their simple life, their way of judging things, their scale of values. And, somehow, their fundamental simplicity and directness in matters of food carries over into the rest of their life, making it a straightforward, healthy, and enjoyable, if very hard, existence.

11. Down to the Sea Again

SO MUCH has already been said in this book about travel that I fear you will begin to think we do nothing else. Well, you would be pretty close to right. As I pointed out earlier, travel is not something the Eskimos do between times, or as an extra fringe on their lives. It is an integral part of their existence. Fishing demands one location during one season of the year. Hunting the seal and whale demands another. Trapping another, and so on. To travel is to live for them, and that is why they have learned to do it leisurely and with relative comfort in their harsh land.

So travel must also be an integral part of the Alaskan missionary's life, especially if he is working with Eskimo villagers. Of dog-team travel I have said enough. Later, I will have much to say about travel by plane. But since we get around a good deal by boat it will not be out of place for me to give you some idea of how we go about it.

The ice had long since disappeared from Kotzebue Sound when I determined to visit the rest of my scattered flock. Those to the east and south I had seen during the winter. Now I would head due north. I would have liked to do it by plane but the farther north you fly, the more expensive the trip becomes. And whatever one might have heard about gold in Alaska, the missionaries are not exactly encumbered with it.

Late one daylight evening the traveling nurse tipped me off that a boat was leaving early the following morning for points north. It took me until after midnight to inveigle a place on board, because of the crowd already signed up. There would be Eskimos and their baggage besides myself, in a thirty-foot converted lifeboat, so you can see that there wasn't much room for swimming pools and salons. I said an early Mass, dashed down to the beach, threw my sleeping bag and Mass kit on board, and away we chugged, with me rather conspicuously ensconced on top of the cabin amidst rope, *uguruk* skins, and what not.

We hadn't gone far out to sea before we passed two whaling boats. The men had evidently had a trying night for they were anchored securely off a sand bar, all sound asleep. During a high wind the night before they had lost a white whale. We had already spied two of their catch anchored prominently in shallow water under a gas-tin buoy to point their location.

This trip of ours was no hurried one. Every camp must be visited. Ours was the first boat north, and tidbits of food, coffee, sugar, and milk, were to be sparingly parceled out along the way. Sheslalik was our first stop. About thirty tents of the Noatakers were pitched in happy disarray among dogs, sleds, skin boats, and drying racks. Many of these people had come here in early spring by dog-team. I could see from the numerous *uguruk* skins pegged out on the clean beach and the abundance of whale meat drying on the racks that they were having a successful season.

Catholics I found were few here. The Quakers looked me over curiously enough, but were quite civil about it. I was called over to visit a Point Barrow Eskimo who had somehow or other wandered down this far. He had perfectly white hair, a rather unusual thing, even for the most aged Eskimo. If I ever met a fine, noble old patriarch, he was it. He was not a Catholic, but had heard much of our faith, and thought well of it. His rare, gentle courtesy and fine hospitality showed him to be every inch a gentleman. But what struck me most of all was his complete absorption in God. Most Eskimos are so completely taken up with the constant fight for existence that they have little time for religion. You have to catch them on the fly. Here was one that had faced all of life's problems squarely and calmly and had found that the answer to them all was living completely for God. His spirituality was entirely unobtrusive, almost like the charming culture that one sometimes sees inherited in old families.

It was probably for that reason that so many of his fellow Eskimos gather around him, just to hear him speak, and ask him questions. As soon as I met him, I felt that here was one I could not teach; rather one from whom I could learn much, and that in my own trade.

As much as I would have liked to stay and visit we could not remain at Sheslalik for more than an hour. We pushed off, and with the boat rising and falling pleasantly on long, even swells we continued on our journey up the coast. Tents were strewn everywhere. Each little inlet revealed a new family or village group gathered where the white fish could be netted best. You see, a straight diet of whale or *uguruk* meat is pretty heavy and the spring run of white fish is ideal to add variety. Then, too, the children could fan out in different directions for duck and goose eggs if the camps were not too close together.

About seven o'clock that evening we rounded the point of Kotzebue Sound and moved out into the Arctic Ocean. Almost immediately the difference in the water became apparent. Here it was cold and crystal clear. Only a few ice floes drifted by us with the current. At Kilikmak we stopped to put off a few passengers and take on others. I stood in admiration at the seamanship of the Eskimo crew. They dropped one anchor about thirty yards off shore and then drifted in until the boat was just out of reach of the breakers. Then they threw out their second anchor.

One squat, stalwart native equipped with hip boots jumped overboard and made the boat doubly safe by anchoring it again, this time to the shore. Then he returned, and without a flicker of expression on his face proceeded to ferry the passengers to shore on his shoulders. Charon had nothing on him.

The people here were new to me, but I went ashore along with the rest. I was pleasantly surprised as I drifted about the camp to see ample signs of Eskimo industry. Of late, rope is scarce in Alaska. Its place is taken by long strands of *uguruk* skin. These are cut circularly around the edge until the whole skin is divided into one long rope. It is then stretched and dried on fish racks. It makes wonderfully pliable rope, and can be used for an indefinite array of purposes.

I saw here one of the few leopard seals I have ever come across. Then just to complete my surprise a little Albino Eskimo lassie skipped playfully down to the beach like a white moth at dusk. Both the government nurse and I were astonished. Among the thousands of Eskimos we had seen, this little girl was the only Albino. I walked a little further and stopped to watch a man making a thirty-foot skin boat. These craft are almost perfect for their uses, but demand constant attention to keep them in proper condition.

Finally the signal was shouted, and we boarded our boat again. By this time the evening twilight was thickening, helped considerably by the fog that rolled in just as we were getting under way. When we finally nosed our way into the narrow channel that leads into the Kivalina Lagoon I could not see for more than ten yards. It was then two o'clock in the morning. We begged the key to the government schoolhouse, and went to sleep therein for about five hours. A different crew was to be mustered here, so I had time in the morning to resume my boy-at-a-circus attitude throughout the camp.

Much to my interest I found out from some Eskimo lads that several flyers' emergency kits had floated ashore in this neighborhood. They were filled with concentrated foods and chocolate. I stood there wondering just where these kits could have come from, crashed Russian planes? American planes lost among the Aleutians? They might even have been carried all the way north from the South Pacific by the Japanese current. I since learned that the Eskimo children have picked up these emergency kits all along the arctic coast.

Off we chugged again, into the fog and rolling sea. There was still a good deal of snow in those parts, giving the air a distinct chill. About nine that night the fog lifted, just as we were passing the tall bluffs of Cape Thompson. Crowbills by the thousands were nesting there so we anchored, and the crew scrambled up the cliffs in search of eggs. Within two hours they were back with over 300 of them, all the size of a large goose egg. Soon a pot was steaming and for the next hour we ate hard-boiled Muire eggs. We shoved off and at about three o'clock in the morning we landed on the clean beach of Tigara.

We were to stay there about three days, so I had ample opportunity to trade ideas with the well-known Archdeacon Frederick Goodwin concerning the conversion of the Eskimo. He has been up here for some twenty years, has translated much of the Anglican Book of Common Prayer into Arctic Eskimo, and has created a little mission that could well be a model for Alaskan missionaries. It is one of the most complete units I have ever seen. The cleanliness of the village, the flourishing native crafts, the religious spirit, all gave real evidence of the good Archdeacon's skill and industry.

My trip back down the coast was a good deal like the one coming up. I held long and frequent discussions, especially with the older Eskimos. It was the first time that most of them had ever seen a Catholic priest and their curiosity reminded me of the Athenian philosophers who asked St. Paul: "May we know what this new doctrine is which thou speakest of? For thou bringest in certain new things to our ears." I made up my mind to return at the first opportunity, and follow up some of the contacts I had made.

That opportunity presented itself the very next year. All my immediate pastoral work had been taken care of during the winter. So, when the S.S. *Waipio* steamed into Kotzebue loaded with the winter's freight for the northern ports, I could not resist the temptation to board her. I was immediately warned that the accommodations were few and not of the best. I just smiled, and thought of my nights in the dripping igloos, and my stormy days in the many sea-beaten small boats I had ridden. Riding in the biggest steamer that had ever entered northern waters was a luxury, no matter how I looked at it.

One friendly young officer expressed concern as to whether or not I would thrive on the plain fare aboard. Even while he asked, he was fondling an orange in his hand. I looked at it and smiled, for I hadn't seen one for over a year. It was no trouble at all to convince him that my physical well-being would run no real danger from the midnight lunches, well-cooked meals, and extraordinarily good food, except, of course, the danger of corpulency.

The steamer itself was anchored some twenty-five miles off shore. It could not even be seen from Kotzebue. So in the wee dark hours of the morning I boarded a local tug, and huffed out into the Sound to the waiting boat. I quickly climbed the ship's ladder and was shown into quite respectable quarters, which included an upper bunk in the pilot's cabin. This grizzled old sea dog looked up through his eyebrows and examined me quietly for several minutes. He had met many priests and preachers in his day, but this one, dressed for the demands of the country and conspicuous for his lack of Roman collar, had him stumped. "Who in hell do you profess to be?" he asked, with all the bluntness that his job had taught him. "Just a two-bit missionary from these parts," I answered.

One thing led to another and before too long I had the very real pleasure of watching this hard-bitten old character chuckling and sighing to himself over a charming life of the Little Flower called *The Rose Unpetaled*. The apparent incongruity between this delicate little saint and the rough old seaman was dissolved in the magic of love. For he fell completely under her spell, and, after long, chill hours of fog and cold wind on the bridge, he would hurry down to his cabin and say, "I must read some more about my little girl."

I had included several books in my luggage; some of a slightly heavier nature, such as Moore's *Dynamic Psychology,* and Aller's *Psychology of Character*. The ship's officers heard of them, and the books started the rounds. Leisure time was all too short to accommodate the resulting discussions. Some of these men were great readers. Some had an insatiable curiosity about Eskimo lore and continually besieged me with questions about their culture, habits, religion, and so forth. All in all, our connection was very interesting; in fact I several times chuckled to myself at finding that I was deep in a religious discussion at one end of a table while a red-hot poker game occupied the other end.

The one thing that struck me about these men was that, in spite of their somewhat electrifying vocabulary, they were absolutely without sham or hypocrisy. They had seen life, and death. This war had made their own lives doubly hard. Like so many of the real Alaskan pioneers, they had known suffering and hardship, but had not succumbed to either.

Up along the coast we pushed. We touched at Kivalina, and

unloaded freight into the Eskimo skin boats that came out to meet the ship. During the time that the ship anchored near the village, gaiety reigned. Old Eskimo women giggled delightedly as they were hauled aboard on the swing to barter their handiwork with the crew. Then came Point Hope. I had been there several times before and was fairly well acquainted with the people. I was invited to spend the night at the Episcopalian mission. The minister in charge was new on the job, and wanted to know much about Jesuit missionary methods with the Eskimo. Later some army and navy men dropped in for a chat, and were surprised to find a minister and a priest discussing religious topics on such a friendly basis. A lively round-table discussion quickly developed in ideal settings. I was called on to state the Catholic position on the invocation of the saints, devotion to our Lady, and several mooted questions on marriage in the Church's history. One of the men present had been trained as a lawyer and used all his training to follow his questions to their source. Happily for all, the discussion continued for several hours on a friendly tone, and I left it feeling satisfied that the results were good.

That night I slept quietly at the Mission, some two miles from the village. During the night a strong wind came up and the ship's officers all returned to their ship in the early morning hours. I was amiably meandering through the village examining the igloos and talking with the natives. I found several old graves entirely fenced in with whale ribs. All of a sudden I noticed for the first time that all the "lightering" had been stopped. I rushed down to the beach, only to find myself marooned. I looked out at the ship, and saw from the position of the flags that it was ready to get under way. Fortunately for me, an army engineer was aboard. He simply had to get ashore to direct an army installation in the neighborhood. I knew that his landing was urgent, so set about getting a boat to take me out, and him in, for the captain had decided to up-anchor and leave within an hour or so.

That was not as easy as it might seem. The waves were rolling high in the wind. The breakers were almost savage. The Eskimos were reluctant to risk their precious skin boats. But finally, almost at the end of the hour, I prevailed on the local Eskimo trader to take me out. We managed to clamber aboard his small tug that was pitching alarmingly, even at anchor. Pulling in two heavy hooks by hand from a heaving deck was never designed as a sedative for jagged nerves. The job was finally done though, and we headed out into the rolling ocean like a paper boat in a storm. By that time I could see that the ship had already lit her running lights, and could hear the anchor chains rattling through the winches. We drew alongside just before she started to move, and I looked up to discover the anxious face of the army engineer peering haggardly over the side. I could almost see visions of court martial or official reprimands etched all over his face. It would have been amusing under less demanding circumstances.

I scurried up the ship's ladder. About halfway up, the mast of the rolling tug rushed by my head, not more than an inch away. A cold chill went down my spine; one inch closer and I would have been dropped with a cracked skull into the icy waters of the Arctic Ocean.

I hardly stepped on the deck when the six hundred feet of anchor chain was finally made fast and we moved northward into the fog and snow. As we sailed out, I looked back at the receding tug and saw the now relieved army officer waving a cheerful good-by from the tossing deck of the tiny boat.

Our course now took us northwest along the extreme tip of Northern Alaska. Point Lay was our destination. We passed the

Cape of Lisborne where old-time whalers used to refuel from the great coal deposits there, and sometimes lay in for the winter. In fog and thickening snow we edged along the dangerous Blossom Shoals where the skeletons of more than one old whaling vessel bear awesome witness to the savagery of this northern sea. Finally we dropped our hook in the rolling waters off Point Lay.

This is a completely Eskimo village. Even the teacher is an Eskimo, which is an unusual thing in Alaska. As we came to rest, a skin sailboat put off from the shore and made its way out to the side of our ship. With a great deal of difficulty the Eskimos aboard made their way over to the lee side, tied up, and clambered up the side. We learned from them that their one and only engine was out of commission, so that lightering the freight in was out of the question unless repairs could be made. The captain sent in his mechanic, but despite all the good intentions in the world, nothing could be done. So we had to up-anchor and leave, after promising the natives there that we would unload their freight one hundred miles up the coast, where they could bring it down overland. Incidentally, Point Lay was the only village in which I did not have the pleasure of saying Mass.

By now we were close to 70 degrees latitude. With the fog, intermittent snow squalls, and a distinct chilling of the air, the crew began to show signs of the northern seaman's jitters. Talk began to deal with the ships they had known that were caught in the ice and had to winter in this forsaken spot; it was not good for morale. One evening as I was standing by the rail looking over the sea, I noticed the white reflection of an ice floe off to the western sky. I kept silent about this, for if I had mentioned it, already stretched nerves would have been further strained.

We landed at Wainright on a Sunday. I arose early, hailed a skin boat, and went ashore to say Mass for the nurse and school teacher. Good weather held for the rest of the day, so we were able to unload the freight in record time.

We left hurriedly, and moved out again. Barrow was sighted a long ways off. It was to be the last stop on the list, the northern-most outpost of Alaska. Would the good weather hold? We had over a thousand tons of freight, and needed every possible break to unload and get out before things closed up tight. We had hardly dropped the hook when a dozen boats came shooting out from the shore. Freighting from ship to shore was well organized here. Every Eskimo knew his job, and did it willingly! Ten-hour shifts were arranged for the crew, and every man, woman, and child from the village was mustered to the work. The piled goods on the beach looked like the supplies of an invasion force. Heavy sacks of flour were labored up from the beach to dry storage by the stocky women. I even saw them rolling heavy drums of oil. In the meantime, I shuttled around, gathered together as many as possible of my flock in the radio station, and said Mass for them there.

Finally another Sunday rolled around, so I picked a spot high in the chartroom of the ship to say Mass for the Catholics among the crew. I was warmed at the sight of these men preparing themselves with special care for Mass. Shaves, clean clothes, shined shoes, all these meant more than they seem in these distant places. It was a thrill for both me and them to have Mass up there, as it were, overlooking the whole earth.

In three days of feverish work the decks were cleared. There was a general sigh of relief as we upped anchor and turned south for the quick trip down the coast. This had been a difficult job, and it was well done. In spite of icy decks and a strong blow,

"My mother's not home!"

Waiting for Cod

"Boys will be boys!"

Fr. O'Connor on the Woodpile

the over-all feeling was — "let her blow and freeze, we're on our way home."

The trip down was fast and uneventful. I had enjoyed the change, and the work with natives who had seldom if ever seen a priest before. It was with real friendliness and reluctance that I waved good-by to the fine men of the crew as they dropped me off at Kotzebue. But I had much to do to prepare for the winter, and my thoughts could not long remain with them as they steamed down Kotzebue Sound and into the outside world.

12. Arctic Flying

SEVERAL times in the course of this book I have mentioned the airplane and what flying has done for Alaska. But merely to mention the word is an injustice. There is so much romance and thrill in the way that arctic flying is done that one would hardly believe it if he had not experienced it himself. Fifty or seventy-five years ago, the Western gunman caught the fancy of American youth in the web of his romance. Today it is, or ought to be, the Alaskan flyer. To risk his life daily, in fact several times daily, to fly impossible weather, to follow the dark curve of a stream through blinding snow at fifty feet elevation, these are normal stakes in the strange game of icy aviation.

Many times I have been more than grateful to these men of the northern skies for their greatheartedness and bravery. They have a code of their own, and part of it is — never let the north-land lick you. Some of them it does lick; some never walk away from one of their many crack-ups. But they have absorbed the sense of trust that the native Eskimo feels about life in general. Trust, or fatalism, I find it hard to distinguish which it is in them.

I remember one case of personal devotion on the part of one of these flyers that will exemplify what I mean. It was the case of Father Tom Cunningham, the pastor of Little Diomede Island, and his friend, Sig Wein. Father Cunningham had been stranded at Wales during the icing fall when the steamer that was supposed to take him and his men parishioners back to their Island after their summer work on the mainland had to leave for Seattle. The derelicts were preparing to try crossing many miles of open sea in small skin boats, when Father Cunningham began to feel dizzy.

As a precaution he consulted a government nurse, who happened to be in Wales at that time. She took his temperature, it was 103. Now this nurse apparently was not a stranger to Alaska. Anyway, she had an ample supply of hard common sense, so Father Cunningham, the man who made up his own mind, went to bed immediately. Chills came, and before long he passed into a state of delirium that caused the nurse and school teachers no little worry and concern. Pneumonia, no respecter of persons, had finally caught up with this man of iron from Little Diomede.

Father Cunningham is an important man in Alaska. The news of his serious illness spread fast. It reached me at Nome. It reached the army camp in Fairbanks, and the flyers requisitioned a Flying Fortress to rescue the patient and bring him into Fairbanks. But the weather was bad. All government planes were grounded. Bill Munz, a crack commercial flyer of Nome, determined to fly anyway. The ceiling was less than two hundred feet — visibility hardly a quarter of a mile through wind-driven snow. Bill took off, and my heart sank as I saw him go. For two solid hours he bucked a head wind. He passed Teller, and near the York Mountains met a solid wall of fog and snow. Disconsolately he turned back, making the return trip before the wind in thirty-five minutes.

Up in Kotzebue, Sig Wein, an Arctic ace if there ever was one, and another personal friend of Father Cunningham heard the news. He was flying two people around on a chartered trip. He rather unceremoniously dumped them off and headed out, straight across the black water and swirling ice floes between Kotzebue and Shishmaref. Everybody up here knows the chance he took. Any engine trouble at all meant certain death in the icy waters of the Arctic. Sig made Shishmaref the first night. Early the next morning in suicidal weather he took off, landed at Wales and taxied right up to the door of the schoolhouse. Father Tom, bundled in a sleeping bag, was loaded on. He hardly knew what was happening, but he did manage to murmur — "I knew you would get through, Sig." Then off they went through a snowstorm to Nome. Over the mountains they ran into wind, fog, and snow so thick that this careful pilot circled for twenty minutes between two mountain peaks waiting for a clearing. He hoped that Father Tom was praying. He must have been, for it cleared momentarily and in they went to Nome. Only the guardian angels of these arctic flyers know how it was done.

Surprise is one of the more romantic qualities of these northern birdmen. You never know when one of them will drop out of the skies at the most unexpected times and places. And they are always welcome.

I remember one trip I was planning to several inland villages. The weather at Kotzebue had been unusually cold, even for the sixth of January. The mercury hovered between 20 and 40 degrees below zero for two months. On the eve of the Epiphany it dropped to a new low, 42 degrees, with a bitter thirty-five mile wind from the west. Cold weather here is not too bad in itself. But cold weather plus a wind — that is miserable, and, incidentally, quite dangerous. This wind could make an unimpeded sweep from Northern Siberia right across the Arctic Ocean straight into Kotzebue.

When I got out in the morning, I did notice that my windmill was turning up 40 amps, but I didn't realize the gravity of the situation until my altar boys came in with frozen ears. Later I learned that several of my Eskimo flock paid the price of their devotion to the three Kings with frozen ears, cheeks, noses, heels, and toes. Rarely do Eskimo children speak of the weather, but that morning they were actually shouting *Allappa!* (My how cold!)

This was the setting for my arranged trip into the interior. I was going by plane, because a dog trip then was impossible, since my jauntings were going to be extensive, and all the local dog mushers were awaiting for a break in the weather to go seal hunting. I was all ready, Blessed Sacrament consumed, water barrel emptied, stuff packed, etc., but at the last minute my plane was requisitioned for a government mission to Nome. I watched it disappear in the distance with no real disappointment, because at the time, I knew it would be used to good purpose against our brethren of the rising sun. Anything can happen here. I was just launching into a profound explanation of the war and all its works and pomps to my Eskimo friends when another plane swung in and landed. I rushed down to the field. It was already late in the day but the pilot graciously offered to take me at least ninety miles into the Kobuk country. I loaded on my sleeping bag and we were off.

It was 40 degrees below zero here on the coast as we rose into the air. The smoke of the village houses was sharply defined in the crystal atmosphere. The cold, bleak outlines of these snowy mountains beneath us were strangely beautiful in the rays of the setting sun. Norvik in the distance was just a smudge of smoke. Up the Kobuk River we flew. I looked down on its tortuous turns which I had toiled over only last year with my dog team. A thin line marked the trail, but no dog team. It was probably 60 below down there, and I shivered when I thought of the twenty-four hours on that trail last year. We covered that stretch by plane in forty-five minutes.

The plane dropped to a graceful landing at Kiana. My pilot took off as soon as I had tossed my sleeping bag and Mass kit to two smiling Eskimo boys. He wished to reach Kotzebue before complete darkness set in. As he swung up into the gathering dusk, and straightened away on his course, I thought of the skill and daring and great generosity of these flying men of the north.

I do believe that most of them fly for the sheer glory of pioneering, that is, the thrill and accomplishment one feels in the constant struggle against these terrifying forces of the northern world. It is not unusual at all to run into winds aloft ranging from sixty to one hundred and five miles an hour. And in the gusty whirlpool air around the mountains, a small plane leaps and drops like a skittish kite. That takes iron nerve, and great, unflagging skill.

I found a little cabin assigned to me by the trader there at Kiana. I was to spend a week. The first night I came near freezing my ears. As soon as the fire went out the cabin became as cold as the outside — 50 degrees below zero. I got up three times during the night to start a new fire. After three days tinkering with a small stove, I finally snagged a drum heater, then I was comfortable.

Kiana is the only arctic village outside of Kotzebue where there are a goodly number of Catholics. There are some fine old sourdough miners here. They have spent the best part of their lives developing gold mines at Klery Creek. Many of them have had sizable fortunes in the past, but instead of withdrawing with their money they sank it back into the ground, and drew a blank. Both the miners and the Eskimos were delighted beyond measure to have a priest with them a whole week. An hour and more was devoted each day to catechism and singing. Daily Mass was well attended despite the excessively cold weather and the distances some had to travel. Those who live in the comfortable atmosphere of the outside, and have to travel a few blocks to church in their cars might be impressed to learn that some of these Eskimos traveled two miles to daily Mass in 52 degree weather — and that fasting!

On the seventh day an aviator friend of mine circled over the village and radioed that he would pick me up the next morning for a still deeper trip into the interior.

That day opened with bitter weather. My flying friend thought he could make it in spite of the driving wind and snow. He got as far as the fringe of the Kobuk Mountains by flying low. All of a sudden his windows blacked out with frost. He was flying blind by sheer instinct. He tried to turn back; one ski caught a jagged piece of ice and was sheared off. In a matter of seconds the other ski went. His wing tipped suddenly, and he hit the snow. With his long arctic training, he automatically shut off the gas line as the plane turned turtle and tossed its engine free. How he and his two passengers ever walked away from that one is nothing short of a miracle.

When the news filtered through to me, I gave up all hope of visiting Shungnak, one hundred miles or so further up the Kobuk River. I was making arrangements to return by dog sled when another wandering plane slid onto the snow with its landing lights all ablaze. It was heavily laded with the persons and equipment of an army lieutenant and sergeant on another government mission.

Since they were going my way, and were quite willing that I accompany them, I managed to squeeze in the next morning. We rose jerkily into the air and made a rough, fast trip across the foothills to Selawick. Here the aviator unloaded his army men and started with me and his mail up into the heart of the Arctic. The wind was strong, but the visibility fine. We flew in between the Baird and Waring mountain ranges. I could look down with comfort and joy on this beautiful Kobuk country.

Forty years ago this region swarmed with miners. One old

timer told me that it had taken him eleven days to go from Kiana to Shungnak. We would make the same trip in just under two hours. Not many miles below I could see a few Eskimo cabins strewn along the trail like discarded lumps of cotton. We passed over Klery Creek. Further along we looked down on Jade Mountain where a fortune could be made by one who is ready to invest a fortune. In the distance was Hunt River, where the Brown Bear and the Black roam undisturbed. I could see, too, Ambler River, with its mineral deposits yet to be developed.

Rough winds shook up the plane as we squared off for a difficult landing at Shungnak. In spite of a dangerous cross wind we slipped onto the snow without even a jar. These flyers can play this wind like an artist plays his instrument; and I was with Sig Wein, Father Cunningham's friend, who is an artist among artists.

I planned to stay several days in this Quaker village, to do what I could with the few Catholics here. One night I was deep in my sleeping bag and I dreamed about Alaskan jade, when I heard a knocking at my door. I glanced at my watch: 3 a.m. I rose and found the fur-bundled construction engineer of the C.A.A. outside. He told me that the cross wind was so strong here that a landing could not be made, and that I was to go overland ten miles up the river where the heavily laden plane could take off directly into the wind.

This engineer had made an all-night dog-team trip to tell me this, and I was very grateful. I dressed, ate quickly, and almost sooner than I can tell it, I was seated in a long, light birch sled sweeping down the steep river bank behind a team of rangy Kobuk dogs. My driver was decked out in a mountain-sheep parka. He was soon to make the trip over the Schwatka Mountains to the north to meet the top-Arctic Eskimos from the Colville section. The Kobuk Eskimo traded rope, tea, *uguruk,* and seal for caribou and mountain-sheep skins. I thought as I listened to his talk how this strangely harsh country really supplies her natives with all they need, if they take the trouble to get it.

Before long we arrived at a government weather station. Here we had a real breakfast. Later we took off in a plane that was so heavily laden that I was surprised that it rose at all. We dropped down to a populous little village called Selawick, and left the C.A.A. men and mail there. I had the plane to myself as we rose again and headed for another northern village to pick up the mail. We worked for altitude to cross the mountains. Off toward the north my gaze ranged unimpeded out over vast expanses of mountains piled upon mountains in endless majesty. As we swept eagle-like over the snowy summits I was more impressed by the strength and vastness of it all than by its cold, silent beauty.

With our landing lights ablaze we slid in on a slough. I gave the people here the benefits of the sacraments and we were off again the following morning. It was not so cold now — only about 10 below. Unlimited visibility gave promise of a fine day in the air. As we topped the mountains I thrilled to see the sun rising in golden splendor. Pilots take the rising sun as just the beginning of another day. To me it is a never ending miracle of power and great beauty.

We picked up mail at two more villages and headed back for Kotzebue. As we neared Kobuk Lake we dipped down for a closer view of the wrecked plane — the one that was to pick me up. It was completely smashed up. Off in the distance we saw a tractor drawing a big bobsled; it was coming from Kotzebue to salvage the wreckage. Then Kotzebue itself. We landed smoothly, and I was back at headquarters.

These flyers and their planes have done much for Alaska. Saving lives by means of emergency flights has become commonplace. They save time on overland flights, but most important of all, they even help to save souls. For example, one day in late spring I was standing before my house, watching the winds whip the sky clean of clouds. Suddenly out of nowhere a plane swooped down and landed. The motor died, the pilot climbed out and walked directly up to me.

"Father, can you be ready in ten minutes? There's a woman dying over in a mining camp, and wants to see you."

Before the plane was gassed up, I was ready with Mass kit and Holy Oils. Off we went. Kotzebue and the lagoon seemed small and insignificant as we mounted into the sky, enlarging our panorama of snow-tipped mountains and endless rolling seas. A good tail wind chased us along to the south. We kept as close to the coast as possible. The beach always affords a fine emergency landing field.

We banked out over Eschscholitz Bay, and I breathed easier when we hit the opposite coast again. The mining town nestled between two steep hills, not a good place to land in a cross wind. We sat down gently, however, and before long I was at the bedside of the dying woman, hearing her confession, and giving her the last sacraments. The Church's sacraments are wonderful everywhere, but here in this lonely and almost savage land, they seem even more wonderful.

Later that evening I was able to gather my flock in the home of my penitent. We said the rosary, and on the following morning I said Mass and gave Holy Viaticum. Someone later remarked that "Viaticum was a sort of a grubstake for heaven." I knew that there was no irreverence meant, and knew, too, that only a miner could see so clearly that Viaticum was actually the food and equipment necessary for the most perilous of all journeys after treasure. Death came quietly for the woman a few days later — and as a striking completion of life's strange circle, I was able to baptize a baby, and give a little girl her first Holy Communion.

With a cross wind still blowing, it was not to be an easy thing for a small-motored plane to climb over the hills. We tried the take-off four times on the trip out, but without success. Several of the miners began to worry about my safety and motioned me from the plane. Incidentally, they were not alone in their worries. With an extra fervent *Memorare* on my lips, I determined on one more try, that was to be all. The pilot kept his eyes glued to the wind sock. The downdraft sometimes twirled it completely around. We might make a tack at the proper moment, and be lifted. This was what actually happened on the fifth try. We staggered at the rim of the hill, caught the full force of the wind, and rose high above the reaching land. With some plane leaps, and accompanying heart leaps, we finally made it back, and I must confess that it felt very comfortable to step out on steady ground again.

It wasn't long, however, before time took the edge off that disturbing experience. I had earned a little extra cash both as weather observer and as bookkeeper for a government engineering project. Since there was nothing in sight for the next week, I determined to use both time and the money to drop down on Nome for a little spiritual refueling among some of my fellow missionaries there.

Plane traveling had become a little spasmodic. This was the time of the year that made insurance companies faint with apprehension. The air was cold, but the Arctic Ocean and the innumerable sloughs were still warm enough to send up clouds of steam that turned to ice almost immediately on contact with the plane. I knew that the careful pilots were more than cagey during this season, so I wasn't sure that I could get a plane to Nome.

Kotzebue weather, however, was good as far as we could see. The wind had swept our field clean, so it really wasn't too much of a surprise when a plane slid in a few days later. I made the necessary arrangements, and took off about an hour later.

I was so busy buckling my safety belt that I didn't notice the rising plane slide and side-step in its ascent. I looked up in time to see the taut jaw and whitened knuckles of the pilot, and realized immediately that we had missed a bad crack-up by inches. The chief engineer, a fellow passenger, later remarked with the laconic unconcern that continual exposure to danger breeds, "You were ten feet from eternity, Father; I measured it myself."

We had gone about fifty miles. In fact, we had just crossed the arctic rim when I began to notice that things looked a little uncertain in the skies ahead. We banked, and skirted some low-lying clouds. It was then that I first noticed the ice on the wings. We were about 4000 feet up, heading out over Eschocholitz Bay. I craned my neck to see the altimeter; we were dropping at the rate of one hundred feet every thirty seconds. I scratched the frost from the side window, and looked down. Black water was coming up pretty fast. I looked ahead; it was 15 miles to the nearest shore. My friend the engineer pointed at the wings; they were well covered with ice by now. Above the roar of the laboring motor, I heard him say something about "prayer." He didn't have to make any suggestions to me; I was already working fairly constantly on that particular matter. I watched the lines of worry forming on the pilot's face, felt the sluggish response of the plane and saw the water coming closer. The land ahead stayed maddeningly distant.

Down, down we sank. I began planning just what I would do when we settled into the water, just as though there would be a chance to survive that deadly ducking. Down, down, we dropped until we were but fifty feet above the waves. Suddenly I realized that the plane had leveled off; we maintained level flight. I saw the pilot's shoulders go up in a sigh of relief. He turned and shouted back at us saying that the ice always cracks off the wings near open water. I shivered a little at the realization of how close we were to having that ice taken off by a plunge in the water itself.

Our immediate destination was Deering. Off in that direction I could see several black snow squalls moving toward us. We swerved and made a bee line for Candle, hidden in a valley between cloud-crowned hills. Long before we reached Candle, snow overtook us. I could see absolutely nothing. The pilot however knew the air currents here, so he rode them in, and without circling swooped in for a quick landing.

We could not delay there at Candle. The field was such that more snow would prevent a wheel plane from taking off. Between snow squalls, therefore, we started down the runway, and took off sluggishly, with a narrow margin to spare. Ten miles of prickly flying brought us into the middle of heavy snow. There is no feeling quite so eerie as flying through snow; absolutely nothing in sight except that continual black gleam of water less than fifty feet below.

I knew that the pilot was following the vague outline of the coast below. Suddenly it dawned on me that this was the anniversary of a fiery crash just a year before. I swallowed rather heavily, and said another prayer. What a fool I was to leave Kotzebue. Between my whispered prayers, I told myself it served me right for having so little sense.

With the wind howling around us, and snow swirling in from the sea, I dimly made out the radio pole at Deering. We missed it by inches. I think I was still holding my breath when we dropped to a quick landing in the deep snow some minutes later.

Only a sense of hypocrisy kept me from dropping on my knees in the snow and thanking God then and there for a safe delivery from that flight. The wind and snow were so furiously blowing that the storekeeper gasped in amazement when we walked in. He had not even heard the roar of our motor as we skimmed above his roof.

The next day was clear. With the help of many Eskimo boys who snowshoed the field ahead of us, we took off and headed for Nome. But the weather again was deceptive. As we neared the big range of the Seward Peninsula we encountered storms which bounced us around. We side-stepped them as much as possible, sliding far off our course in the process. As we roared over Death Valley, I looked down and thought a little grimly how well the place was named. What a job it would be trying to get away from a forced landing there!

To get in to Nome, we had to swing one hundred miles to the east, go around Council, and finally enter Nome from the south. The weather was much warmer on the south of the mountains. No snow at all; in fact a ski plane could not have landed.

Just before we arrived at Nome a formation of P-40's roared up to meet us. With their blinding speed they made our little commercial kite look like a lumbering barge. They moved around us a couple of times, and then were off with a friendly and courteous wave of the pilots' hands. And then Nome. My missionary colleagues were somewhat taken aback with the warmth and enthusiasm with which I greeted them later — wondered if I were a little delirious. "Just glad to be here," I explained; and spent an hour or two relating the details of the trip down, not a little of which was sheer praise for the cool efficiency of my pilot through some exhaustingly difficult flying.

I personally owe much to these flying men of the north; my people owe them much. And I shall always be grateful for what they have done; I shall continue to show that gratitude by praying God to keep their wings and hearts clean and sure in the northern air.

13. Surprise!

IN THE fifteen years and more that I have spent in Alaska there is one thing that is continually impressed on my mind. It is summed up in the old New England saying: "It ain't what it's cracked up to be." The decision to leave the relative comfort of the United States to spend one's life in a new and proverbially harsh land, among a strange, Oriental people, is not an easy one. But, true to the old New England aphorism quoted above, things have turned out so differently from what I had expected that my turn up here has been replete with surprises — many of them pleasant ones.

One of the first, and most soul filling of these surprises was the scenery on the trip up. For some time I had explored the ship, filled with eagerness for my new job, and yet possessed of a nameless fear of the unknown. But both concerns soon faded in the absolute glory of that trip. I began to be treated to such scenic wonders that my mind finally became confused and ceased to catalog them. After a while I could only stand motionless in the bow of the ship and just look, and wonder. The giant stillness seemed to roll out from the coastal mountains like waves of peace. There were forests; acres, miles of green-black untouched forests stretching away like undulating oceans of dark color to an horizon of startling blue. There were strange formations of clouds, all in a white that made the blue background only more startling. There were the sudden inlets in the coast line with their deep, cliff-like descent to the clear waters. The brilliant white of a ribbon of sand that occasionally flashed out at the foot of the dark shoreline. "Mountains piled upon mountains"; glaciers whose gigantic scope and power were faintly hinted at when a piece of ice as big as a city block broke off and crashed into the sea, rocking our ship a mile away. And the air! Nothing could give an adequate impression of the clarity of that air. Individual pine needles seemed to stand out against their blue backgrounds. To breathe deeply was to feel the fingers of new life reaching deep down into one's very being.

That went on and on, until I found myself rejoicing to see that the sun took longer and longer to sink below the horizon. Each day gave me more time to take in the splendors that surrounded me. It was so much more than I had ever expected.

And from that day to this, it has been the same. Many people, I know, have come to Alaska, attracted by the greatness of the country. Most of these newcomers cannot help thinking that Alaska has the proportions of a mighty nation; its climate is varied (to say the least), its riches abundant, its scenery magnificent. But so many of the *cheeckakos,* or tenderfeet, suffer from one implacable disease before long. It is the disease of disillusionment; or, to go "New England" again, they find out that "it ain't what it's cracked up to be."

That is true, of course, in two ways. It is not as great or as promising as it seemed to be; or it is not as difficult as it looked from a distance.

Some find out, for instance, that ice and snow, northern lights, and midnight suns are not to be had for the wishing. It is true that those who have lived for years in Alaska have seen these things, but they have frequently paid well for the sight. Old sourdoughs cannot help talking about these beautiful sights of the North. They are as human as the rest of us. By dint of continual repetition, and occasional embroidery, they turn the unusual into the merest commonplace, and vice versa. The long leisures of the northern winters are fertile ground in which these old-timers can cultivate prosaic stories into strange and exotic tales.

Visitors, therefore, are frequently loathe to believe that the blizzards do not rage during the summer; that midnight suns are confined to the short period of one month; that bear hunts are off the beaten trail of things done, and require time and money to make them. Then, too, the northern lights cannot be turned off and on at a tourist's whim. Even Mt. McKinley, North America's highest peak, is rather modest. I have known photographers to wait weeks in vain for a good "pose."

But the climate and scenery does not yield any more inverse surprises than do the people. The newcomer finds that the blandly moon-faced Eskimo speaks intelligent English. They handle a hammer and saw with remarkable skill. They take clocks, engines, and radios apart and actually get them together again. They barter their fur with Oriental smoothness and keenness. They think nothing of building up two to five hundred dollars' worth of credit, and actually boast about it.

Astonishing, too, is their talent both in Church and in school — when they want to perform. The average youngster has a fine memory. He can be taught both chess and bridge. But when it comes to games his inventive and individualistic mind comes to the fore and rules are eventually changed to fit his whims and temperament. Baseball regulations will be followed politely as long as a few whites are around to insist on their observance. When the Eskimo is left to himself, however, he does away with the rules and indulges his instinct for the bizarre and the flexible.

Punctuality at school is a virtue which each successive teacher insists on in vain. Eventually, Eskimo lads and lassies win out, and begin to show up when they feel like it. As a matter of fact, the weather, good hunting, lack of wood, fishing, and other distractions of life are constantly offering plausible escapes from the boredom of the classroom. Needless to say the youngsters are shrewd diplomats, and are not slow in making full use of the slightest reason for missing school.

A fairly strict adherence to Catholic liturgy and doctrine takes years to assimilate and finally practice. St. Paul's injunction to women to keep their heads covered in church, despite frequent admonitions by the pastor, is considered a little thing, and just as often as not is forgotten. Regular Sunday attendance at Mass under pain of mortal sin is taken with a grain of salt. As for eating fish on Friday, well, every day is fish day in Alaska, so when meat comes, it is eaten on Friday or any other day! In fact, many forget all about Sunday during a week of bad weather when every day is a holiday from the tasks that keep these people alive. In the country where the fishing comes with a rush and stops just as suddenly, incidentals such as night or day, Sunday or weekday do not mean a thing. Unloading boats, too, must be done in a rush. Skippers fear these intemperate zones, with the ice floes as sudden and stealthy as they are.

The easy flow of life in set and well-organized time patterns is simply not a point of consideration for the Eskimo. He is first and foremost an opportunist. The fundamental instinct of self-preservation is so well developed in him that other considerations matter little if at all. He works solely for this end. Unfortunately he does not believe in conserving or hoarding. What he has he uses immediately. The surplus is given away. The result is that with nothing on hand he is constantly alert for a fresh supply of necessities. His leisure or inactivity is reserved for periods of bad weather or sickness. When a white and Eskimo mix, all these differences immediately come to the fore, and they proceed successfully to misunderstand one another. The white calls the Eskimo "lazy, improvident"; the Eskimo wonders in his silent way why the white, with so much, is always grasping for more.

Aside from the people, the land itself holds the most startling surprises. Its coast line stretches for thousands of miles of bays, inlets, lagoons, and breath-taking fiords. Its waters hold more fish perhaps than the whole coastal area of the States combined. A variety of rivers, from shooting mountain torrents and cataracts, to the broad, deep channel of the Yukon which is longer than the Mississippi, network the land. There are plains and swamps, mountains and foothills. To put it simply, the country is vast and rugged, waiting for a strong and rugged people to populate it; a people that Robert Service spoke about:

> *Send me the best of your breeding, lend me your*
> *   chosen ones;*
> *Them will I guild with my treasures, them will I*
> *   glut with my meat;*
> *But the others, the misfits, the failures — I trample*
> *   under my feet.*

With all its natural wonders and inducements to wealth, northern Alaska is nevertheless hard on city-bred men. Life is lonely, companionship is sketchy, amusement as the city gives it is almost nonexistent. The bigger towns have them, but not the smaller villages, and it is to these that people must go to make and develop Alaska.

I have seen men and women wrecked in one winter. They come up here with the best intentions in the world. The government might have supplied them with good quarters, too, but somehow or other they gradually went downhill. Long winters, the confinement that always accompanies blizzards and extreme weather, lack of interest in local affairs; it is hard to put one's finger on the exact difficulty, since there may be a host of them.

Anyway, they just do not fit. A reaction sets in. Sparkling optimism ends in drab pessimism, and they find it necessary to move, or to be moved.

However, with all these difficulties, hard labor, protracted leisure, no mail, sudden emergencies, the most difficult element of this northern life is isolation.

Isolation is a dreadful thing to most people. It seems to connote all that is lonely and abandoned. It is an emptiness, a vacuum, that draws on the outer walls of the soul until they collapse like the sides of a vacuumed tin can.

Fortunately there are different kinds of isolation. It is one thing to be isolated in your own home and in a place you love; it is quite another to be alone far from home. The isolation of a frontier settlement has a charm all of its own if it is rightly considered. The civilization of the crowded cities and their mechanical luxuries may be far away, but not the initiative, the hardihood, and the rough friendliness of the pioneer. Living much in the open and matching wits against the forces of nature give life a fullness and contentment which city dwellers nervously seek, but seldom find.

For example, one morning this past winter, a particularly cold one (more than 40 below zero), I slipped out into the dark village on skis. All around me the huts were buried in snow, ghostly mounds looking like ancient tombs. It was hard to believe that each house covered big families, all asleep, quiet and warm. Only one light shone bright and clear at the far end of the village. Everything else was dark and deathly still. The skis barely whispered as they slipped over the hard snow.

I have often noticed that whenever I bear Holy Viaticum with me, the dogs treat me with a distinct courtesy. They either stand at attention as I pass, or gaze in silence from the seclusion of their quarters. Usually an Eskimo dog does not like the smell of a white and voices his disapproval in no uncertain terms. This morning as I carried the Blessed Sacrament with me I passed the huge Siberians that I occasionally borrow to pull me on skis. They are always yapping to go when I approach them. But now even they were as silent and respectful as monks, though, incidentally, they were doubly noisy on my return trip.

When I entered the hut where the solitary light had been burning, I found everything in readiness; table prepared, candles set, even the *Confiteor* was being recited quietly by the family in Latin. Devoutly the aged father received his Lord in Holy Viaticum. Prayers were said in hushed tones, and a few quiet words of gratitude were spoken by the family. Once more I was outside in the solitude. I circled around a bit on the way home, the longer to reflect and pray on the mystery of love I had just witnessed and the one I was witnessing all about me. For there is something magnetic about the arctic darkness, something that draws prayer from the soul like a giant magnet, when only the stars seem awake, and hang so low that you can reach up and touch them. The silences fairly pulse around you. Here was isolation, too, but more the beauty of solitude.

But the old Alaskan isolation is gradually being smashed by the roar of the airplane. And with it, I fear, a healthy independence is also being destroyed. The Eskimo used to be the freest of men. His clothing and food came from his own land and was produced by his own ingenuity. There were no such things as middle men in his life. The plane has brought him three things that are causing a violent change; gas and electric machines, the radio, and the movies. These "improvements" can undoubtedly bring ease and enjoyment into the Alaskan life, but they can also bring a very real slavery. The Eskimos won't know it until it is too late. It takes time for a primitive people to adjust themselves to our modern life. For example, the young men were drafted lately for army life. Eight out of every ten men drafted from around Kotzebue had to be sent home, and they, in their simple way, could not realize why they were incapable of being assimilated. They are used to isolation of a certain type and need the independence that it gives them. But now we find the plane everywhere rushing things at them which are breaking down their independence, much too fast.

All this is not to say that the Eskimos should not have progress or improvement. But dumping the products of a highly mechanized civilization into the lives of a primitive people does not bring progress and improvement. Things in themselves, luxuries, machines, movies, and so forth, these do not mean improvement, necessarily. This is particularly true when they come from the outside and are not by-products of the people's native ingenuity. The Eskimos are fascinated by all the new inventions which modern life has brought to them via the plane, but they do not know how to fit them into their lives without upsetting long-standing systems of values. As a result they see the defective sides of modernism and not the real usefulness of practical inventions.

Sending a plane winging into the deep isolation of the North can be a blessing. It can bring medical assistance, transport people to hospitals, bring in needed supplies with no waste of time, and in general triumph over the vast stretches of difficult terrain which make Eskimo life so taxing. But it can also bring alcohol, germs, and cheap commercialism which will ruin the Eskimos as a people. Lots of Americans would find this a surprising thing, I know. They imagine that to bring all the modern developments to the Eskimos is the kindest way to treat them. That is because they do not know what a primitive people is like; and also, I strongly suspect, because they think that isolation is a fearsome thing in itself. They do not realize that at times it can be beautiful, ennobling, and sometimes even necessary. It has gone into the making of the Eskimo character as much as anything else. So, surprising as it might seem, these natives of the North present the sobering picture of a people being killed with the misguided kindness of a mechanically superior civilization.

14. Mushing for God

IT IS almost a truism to say that this land grows on one. It has been said so often, and under such varied circumstances that I hesitate to repeat it. As a matter of fact, though, there is not much else one can say about his experience in the North over a period of years. As was mentioned in the previous chapter, it is perhaps the continual surprise of life in the North which keeps the place growing on one.

For even the hardships themselves are surprising. They are not actually as bad as I had feared. Take the matter of food, for instance. It is true that there cannot be all the culinary color that one might wish under more favorable circumstances, but things could be very much worse indeed. I remember my fears about the fish diet, its unending monotony. Yet I have found out from actual experience that my table in winter can be varied without difficulty by ptarmigan, willow-grouse, reindeer steak, and sometimes moose. In spring and fall, duck and goose offer a pleasant change. The Eskimo has a much wider variety, of course; but then, his taste buds and imagination are much hardier than mine.

Personally, I have found the lack of fresh vegetables my greatest gastronomic difficulty. And even in this department, we get along pretty well. At Holy Cross Mission on the Yukon we produce potatoes and turnips in abundance. At Akulurak up near the Bering Sea we raise lettuce, radishes, and turnips. We can keep potatoes and turnips all winter, supplemented when the cash drawer allows with canned vegetables of various kinds. So it really isn't so bad as it might seem, after all.

There is one hardship of the North, however, that is a reverse surprise — the two seasons, before the breakup, and before the freeze-up, i.e., May, June, and around October. Repeatedly the mail fails to get through, travel is at a standstill, chilling rains and wind become the order of the day. In fact, almost everything blends harmoniously together in a veritable symphony of depression. The only cure for this spell that I have discovered is hard work and a definite schedule. Without a schedule one will soon ᴅe "shaking hands with the willows," as the saying goes.

Surprisingly enough, winter is really not as bad as it sounds; and summer can be much worse than it sounds. There is one deadly serious enemy of summer bliss, and he is enough to cloud out any of the other advantages of climate and scenery. I speak of the mosquito, the master of the summer season. By millions, they swarm up from the numberless sloughs and lakes of the melting tundra, attacking front, flank, and rear, anything that is warm and has blood. I have known deer to run against the wind for days in an attempt to escape his torture. And man; well, the Eskimo, with his Oriental placidity, takes it; and the white tries to conquer, by smudges, nets, powders, and poisons. Neither is quite successful in his method of dealing with the problem. Even the tough Malemute, that can stand days on the trail and incalculable cold, even he surrenders to the pest of summer, whimpering plaintively under his attack. For this enemy does not bring death; that is a consummation too sweet to be hoped for. He takes life's blood, and leaves poison for his payment.

Winter, of course, has its difficulties, but they can be overcome. This can be done on one condition, namely, that the white follows the advice of the native who has spent his life learning to overcome those very difficulties. Life is short — and not very sweet — for the white who allows his impatience and superiority to scorn the unprepossessing blandness of the Eskimo teacher.

Straw, for instance, is a very humble thing. There are a thousand reasons for throwing it away, and for laughing at the man who saves it jealously. Yet heaven help the white who laughs at the Eskimo use of straw.

I have mentioned Eskimo ingenuity before. When he applies it to the matter of straw the results are wonderful to behold. There are many varieties of tundra grass up here, and I need not say that they all look alike to my foreign eye. Not so to the dimming eyesight of the old Eskimo grannies. They can go out in the fall and return with their arms loaded with a special variety of hard, fiberlike grass that they patiently weave into huge, egg-shaped baskets.

But here at the Mission, and among many of the Eskimos themselves, the principal use of straw is for footware. We have a special house set aside to store our straw and to keep it dry during the winter. It is cut after it has been thoroughly seasoned by the wind and frost. Much is needed, for it is put to almost daily use in packing the boots of a hundred children. It is rounded and shaped to fit the size. Of course, a larger boot can be made into a snug fit by the simple introduction of more straw. It makes an excellent cushion for the foot, besides giving the warmest possible protection against the cold. And that is a protection of which one must take advantage because frost-bitten feet are as effective demobilizers as any other sickness.

Another thing the white must learn from the Eskimo is extreme care of his boots, or *mukluks*. It really takes a woman to care properly for the Eskimo *mukluk*. On the trail I invariably hand over my hip-length seal-skin boots to an old grandmother. In doing this I know that my boots will be dried, softened, and

re-strawed by the next day. It is imperative to have your boots
in good condition when you are going to be exposed to bitter
and penetrating cold for eight or nine hours at a time. I know
by experience what misery is in store for the tundra traveler
who has failed to heed the Eskimo's warning about this particular use of straw.

And then, too, straw is used extensively in the igloos themselves. Not long ago I stopped in one that had nothing but a
dirt floor. I foresaw a chilly night on that cold ground. My
host, however, was equal to the situation. After I had finished
my instruction and night prayers with the family, a thick straw
matting appeared from nowhere and was rolled out on the floor
for my convenience. I slept warmly and soundly. The following
morning when we opened the door the cold air rolled in like
steam. It was going to be bad traveling. I turned and noticed
my host and traveling companion slipping on a cleverly made
straw oversock. He assured me that a rabbit sock was not equal
to the warming qualities of the ones he was using.

The native can also teach the average white much about
handling dogs. And it is well to learn this, and learn it carefully.

For a man's life depends on his dogs if he has to travel in
the winter. And he must get to know them. He must realize
that in the early winter season the Malemutes are impatient with
months of inactivity, and often express their impatience with
murderous dogfights. Then, too, in making teams, friendly dogs
must be paired, because a fight is like a fire; it can spread with
swift destruction. And eleven brutes, seventy-five pounds each
of whirling, snarling, slashing devilishness, all piled in a squirming mass of mayhem, can cause an anxious moment or two.

Experience, if one survives it, and a willingness to learn from
the natives are the two things that will make winter part of
one's life, and not the end of it. Many a confident *cheechako*

has come to Alaska intent on teaching the "dumb" Eskimo a thing or two. He is a happy man if he lives long enough to learn how to learn.

And then the weather. One must learn to gauge it nicely. Certain signs show a storm. And when a storm is rising, then one gets a chance to drive the difficult virtue of patience deep in his soul. He can never be in a hurry, because no man alive can conquer an Alaskan storm in its fury. For that fury carries with it the blindness of blankets of snow, exhaustion, and most deadly of all, cold. Quiet cold is not difficult to stand. When it goes on the march, though, be careful. On the coast, where the air is damp, two parkas are not enough to keep out the deadly searching of its chilly fingers. So, with the unconcern of a philosopher, I have long since learned to imitate my natives, and arrange my trips to avoid such weather if it is at all possible. My natives will wait with complete contentment for five or six days for the weather to turn. That is why so many of them reach middle age.

Dog mushers as a rule prefer cold weather for traveling. Soft weather frequently comes up from nowhere in the midst of a long trip. The soft sticky snow can wreak havoc on some poor lagging Malemute, turning him from a proudly flag-waving conqueror of the white, into a dragging, whimpering bundle with dejected fur and sore feet. The best season for travel is the latter part of March and April. Fifty miles a day can be covered then in almost any direction. The snow is crusted, the dogs are hardened, and daylight stretches far into the night.

In moving across the winter tundra one does not come upon igloos built exclusively of snow and ice, as is so often pictured to youthful imaginations. I have mushed up and down the Yukon and Kuskokwim for hundreds of miles; during the past sixteen years I have haunted the wastes near the Bering Sea, and the

Arctic Ocean, and I have yet to see an igloo built entirely of snow and ice. Dwellings on the big rivers are built of logs. In the tundra they are made of mud and timber. In other words, they are very much like farmers' root cellars. The entrance is sometimes arched with snow as a windbreak.

In winter these dwellings are completely covered with snow, making them airtight and easily warmed with little wood, and sometimes with body heat alone.

Although the winter is long and arduous it has its rare, blissful moments. "Mail" is the magic, solacing word which can enhance a dull, winter day. Mail actually does arrive in the far points of the north. And when one considers the circuitous route, the numberless re-sortings, and the various modes of travel involved, it is another source of arctic surprise that mail arrives at all. Letters are seldom lost en route, although the question of time hardly enters into consideration. And the gentle handling of parcels is an improvement which is yet to be hoped for in these parts. A package, unless carefully prepared, will arrive in a state beyond recognition.

That is easy to understand if one considers some of the rather astonishing facts of the case. Alaskan mail is sorted first in *Seattle*. From this port it goes by boat to *Seward*. From *Seward* it is taken by train to *Nenana*. Lower Yukon mail is here re-sorted and taken down river as far as *Fortuna Lodge*. A Bering Sea tug takes it on down river for points along the coast and the Delta. What is left of the mail is then thrown on the Mission Diesel and finally ends its long and varied trek.

In winter this hegira is even more varied. Train, boat, plane, all play their part. Two relays of dog teams form the last stage. In late winter with a well-broken trail the transit by dog team may be as smooth as that by rail. But in early winter or over a rough trail, the trip is one series of unpredictable surprises.

Again, patience is in order. Sometimes by a rare stroke of fortune a letter may arrive only two weeks away from the sender. Three weeks or a month is the usual thing. Not infrequently an important letter will be two months en route, especially during freeze-up and breakup periods. If the letter demands an immediate answer, as some correspondents do with refreshing naïveté, the sender better settle himself back comfortably for a wait of approximately three months. Incidentally, too, a parcel-post package may wander around with informal abandon anywhere between one and six months. I have often received two letters in the same mail, the later-dated asking urgently why I had not answered the first. But with some uncanny inevitability bills seem to slip through all the obstacles the mail system might place before them with unconcerned ease. They infallibly make good connections at every postal junction.

However, no matter how informal may be the mail's wanderings, its arrival is always as welcome as the first flowers of spring. One has only to experience the absence of the mail team to realize what an important factor it plays in the life of the Mission. The kids, of course, are always the first to sight the approaching mailman. They can distinguish it as the mail team even while the dogs and sled are nothing but a slim black line on the white horizon of the tundra. Their cries bring out the whole staff of the Mission. Quick-fingered Eskimo lads are ready to grab the panting Malemutes and lead them away from the jealous huskies of the Mission kennels. Our dogs have never become friendly with those vicious intruders. Six hundred pounds — the mail sled limit — is whisked indoors in the twinkling of a northern light.

First-class mail is, of course, of overpowering interest. Here, true to form, those long, sleek letters with the address peeping through glazed windows on their faces are the easiest to detect.

These unpaid bills are always put aside with a sigh to await the stronger sinews of prayer and quiet.

Letters from home and friends are immediately devoured. Then those ebullient epistolary creations telling the hard-working missionary how he can make a fortune without turning his dogs' hair are duly filed away — in the wastebasket. There is generally a letter or two from some curious stranger inquiring about the personal habits of the Eskimo; does he smoke? Drink? How are his morals? What is his history? Background? Environment? Future development? All those simple little questions that would demand a series of volumes to answer. But I try to do my best.

At times a substantial check may be tucked within the pages of a modest and encouraging letter — one of the more deeply touching of my surprises. And then it is that my throat fills, and my never slackened wonder at God's providence and man's kindness rises up in its glorious colors to blind me for a moment.

But God's providence and man's kindness must continually combat the bleakness and desolation of these northern wastes. Outside my team is ready, the dogs are barking impatiently, and I must go.